1993

To Jan

I did enjoy ... ay

the Lord bless ...

His care.

with ... ar

Elaine

The Comi

The Coming Revival

Colin Urquhart's Vision

Melanie Symonds

■ Highland Books ■
Guildford, Surrey

British Library Cataloguing-in-Publication Data. A catalogue record for this book is available from the British Library

Published by Highland Books, an imprint of Inter Publishing Service (IPS) Ltd, 59 Woodbridge Road, Guildford, Surrey GU1 4RF.

Typeset by The Electronic Book Factory Ltd, Fife.
Printed in the UK by HarperCollins Manufacturing, Glasgow.

ISBN No: 0 946616 93 0

Acknowledgements

I would like to thank Colin Urquhart for his teaching and for the complete freedom I had in writing this book; thank you also to the whole Kingdom Faith team who showed their support and encouragement.

Dedication

To Elizabeth Allan and Elizabeth Scofield,
who faithfully prayed for me while I was writing.

Contents

INTRODUCTION

On 24th September 1991, just six days after I had been interviewed and accepted as a Kingdom Faith student, I went to the usual Tuesday evening celebration meeting at Roffey Place and, while there, heard a prophecy about revival. Earlier that day the publisher of this book had telephoned to ask whether there was the possibility of my writing anything while I was a student at Roffey. At the time the significance of the prophecy's timing in connection with this book did not strike me, although I was careful to record it in the back of my Bible. It came from an Australian, John Lee, a worship leader and songwriter visiting England:

> 'God is saying we must be ready for the greatest revival ever. There are three main areas we must work on:
> Firstly, we need to be *people* of the *presence* of God. This should be our prayer:
> Lord, launch and birth us into something deeper and more true than we've known before. Draw us into you through Jesus.
> Secondly, we need to be people of *purity*, so we can be people of power. Then we can receive the wind of power which will blow away those who have not humbled themselves.
> Our prayer is:
> Lord, help us choose to walk in purity.
> Thirdly, we need to pray and intercede for *revival*.
> Pray: Revive us, Lord, and save our land.'

Chapter One

FOLLOWING THE VISION

Looking at Britain today, once a God-fearing country which has enjoyed revivals in the past, it is easy to say it needs a massive social, political and moral overhaul. The state of Britain can be compared with the moral and economic crises which visited biblical Israel as a result of her rebellion against God's laws:

> 'Now therefore, O our God, the great, mighty and awesome God, who keeps his covenant of love, do not let all this hardship seem trifling in your eyes ... In all that has happened to us, you have been just; you have acted faithfully, while we did wrong. Our kings, our leaders, our priests and our fathers did not follow your law; they did not pay attention to your commands or the warnings you gave them.' (Nehemiah 9:32–34)

Many believe that the turmoil spoken of in the prophecy has already begun, with an economic chaos to follow which will be fuelled by self-interest.

Yet there is light in the darkness. Colin Urquhart and other leading Bible teachers believe that God's will for Britain is revival.

Some believed that the charismatic renewal was in itself a worldwide revival, but it did not arouse the same interest the full-blown demonstrations of the Holy Spirit's power as seen in great historic revivals. Its impact on the nation's morals and institutions has been negligible. Sadly it never grew into revival, and by the early 1990s it seemed as if some sections of British Christianity were on hold. Indeed, the Church of England has been actively planning for shrinkage, proposing to close theological colleges while strenuously debating whether or not to ordain women.

While the nation's media, disillusioned after the materialistic 1980s, showed increasing interest in the occult and supernatural, the Church has not been in a position to give decisive leadership.

Colin, amongst others, saw that in spiritual terms Britain was groaning under the 'yoke of the oppressor' (Isaiah 9:4); this oppression has materialised as economic uncertainty and unemployment, a 33 per cent divorce rate, child abuse, drug addiction, homelessness and freely available abortion and pornography amongst other social ills. In other words, Britain has manifested all the symptoms of a society determined to please itself, whose citizens are encouraged to put themselves before others, certainly not allowing God into their lives.

Now, Colin believes, God wants to restore spiritual leadership to Britain in the same way that it once enjoyed economic supremacy, so the coming revival will overflow from Britain to Europe and America.

While waiting for this to happen, Christians are called to be 'leaven in the lump', in readiness for a glorious spiritual transformation which will affect every level of society, because revival will produce a fear of the Lord (Isaiah 11:3), who is no respecter of persons.

It is not fanciful to pray for a truly Christian Prime Minister, and for other members of the government to be born again and filled with the Holy Spirit. Since the autumn of 1992 Colin has believed that this is one of God's instructions to lay the foundations of revival.

Key prophetic words for the pre-revival period come from Isaiah.

> 'The people walking in darkness have seen a great light; on those living in the land of the shadow of death a light has dawned. You have enlarged the nation and increased their joy; they rejoice before you as people rejoice at harvest, as men rejoice when dividing the plunder. For as in the day of Midian's defeat, you

have shattered the yoke that burdens them, the bar across their shoulders, the rod of their oppressor.' (Isaiah 9:2–4)

Colin is one of those who teaches that Scripture has three applications: firstly in its historical context (this prophecy referred to the birth of Jesus), secondly as a reference to the end of the world, and thirdly when it is brought home anew to our spirits by the Holy Spirit.

He enlarges upon Isaiah's theme:

'When the light shines in the way that God desires among His people, the Kingdom of God is extended in the land. There is an increase of joy, not just among the people who receive the light, but in the nation. They rejoice because of the harvest of souls that is taking place, while the yoke that had burdened them individually and nationally is being shattered!'

And what will break the yoke? Only an anointing from God:

'In that day their burden will be lifted from your shoulders, their yoke from your neck. The yoke will be broken because of the anointing oil.' (Isaiah 10:27, NKJV)

The anointing is not something God's people can manufacture, and it is certainly not the same thing as a call. Yet God is not withholding His revival; rather, as we open up more of our lives to Him, so He is able to pour in more of His anointing to overflow to others. In other words, we need to start with nothing less than personal revival.

Since 1976 Colin has taught congregations that God wants to bring in revival through them, that He is raising up a holy people for Himself. Their holiness will not be of the ivory tower variety; it is their relationship with God and with one another which will set them apart as holy. Having met with God in His holiness, they will demonstrate the same desire as Jesus had to be intensely involved with those around them as they spread the good news of God's Kingdom. In the same way that the lifestyle of the early apostles found them favour with the rest of Jerusalem (Acts 2:47), so the empowered lifestyle of today's apostles will make an impact on the rest of the nation. In 1979 the German evangelist Reinhard Bonnke was convinced that Britain was approaching her season for revival:

'As surely as the sun is shining – God is going to pour out His Spirit on these isles.'

For Colin Urquhart, each of the last decades has had its own characteristic – and the word from God he has proclaimed has been constant. In 1984 he wrote:

> 'The seventies was a decade of renewal; the eighties a decade of evangelism. The nineties will be a decade of revival. There has been a growing expectation that we shall see a sovereign move of God's Spirit in revival power. It is easy for people to become excited about revival and to engage in wishful thinking. But I believe the prophetic word of the Lord is that we shall move into a revival situation in the near future.'[1]

What is revival? Here is one recent definition:

> 'A revival is a sovereign outpouring of the Holy Spirit upon a group of Christians resulting in their spiritual reviving and quickening, and issuing in the awakening of spiritual concern in outsiders or formal church members; an immediate, or, at other times, a more longterm, effect will be efforts to extend the influence of the Kingdom of God both intensively in the society in which the Church is placed, and extensively in the spread of the gospel to more remote parts of the world.'[2]

'A going of God amongst His people' is how the Scottish islanders around Lewis described the extraordinary events of the late 1940s when people stumbled into the police station in amazed confusion after meeting God on the open road. Others would row for three hours to reach a prayer meeting on the other side of a lake.

The Welsh revival at the turn of the century is also well known. In fact, every area of Britain has experienced revival at some time or other – except Sussex. And according to Colin, who was called to base his ministry in West Sussex, that is about to change as he and his team single-mindedly prepare for revival.

Colin's ministry

It was certainly not Colin Urquhart's idea to become a national speaker when, as a nervous 23-year-old, he obeyed God by being ordained in 1963.

Yet since 1970, when he saw miracles become commonplace in his church in Luton, he has been aware that he is one of those whom God will use to usher in 'the greatest movement of God's Spirit that we could imagine taking place in this nation'.

Having lived in revival, albeit local rather than national, he knows the real thing. His church in Luton became famous after his first book, *When the Spirit Comes*, recorded extraordinary blessings, miracles and healings. The depth and extent of change amongst his congregation later proved to him that this awakening was not renewal, but revival.

'At St Hugh's it had been revelation for people to realise that they could pass from death to life *now*; that they could receive the gift of eternal life *now*; that they could know Jesus personally *now*; that their lives could be filled with His power, His love, joy and peace *now*; that He would bring His healing into lives *now*.'[3]

After five years Colin reluctantly left St Hugh's, knowing that God was calling him to fulfil a national preaching ministry in response to the many invitations he was receiving. A proper base was required, which was provided a year later at The Hyde in Sussex, where the ministry was transformed 'explosively' by another ten-month period of God's revival power. He believed God had promised him that this time was a foretaste of the revival to come in Britain, and that his ministry would be at the heart of events. One frequently used prophetic analogy likened the ministry to the tip of an arrow, breaking through into revival.

Obedience to God's calling has ensured a life which has never been dull for Colin and his family. Over the years others have become involved in this and other ministry ventures, but as there is not the room here to faithfully record each arrival and departure, the following timetable shows the Urquhart family's movements:

1970 The Urquharts move to St Hugh's, Luton, the third church Colin worked in, his second as vicar.

1975 Just after Christmas they leave for a temporary ministry base at East Molesey.

1977 The family moves to The Hyde, the new ministry base at Handcross, West Sussex.

1982 The Urquharts move out of The Hyde to their own extended household at nearby Bolney.

1983 In January Colin tells the fellowship they are to buy a training college, Roffey Place; by November the necessary £600,000 has been provided.

1984 1st January: Roffey Place opens its doors to students.

1986 The lease on The Hyde is relinquished.

1988 Colin's house at Bolney is sold and he moves to Colgate, a village nearer to the college.

1989 Colin and his family sell their Colgate house and move into the old house at Roffey Place, where he becomes full-time College Principal.

1991 Kingdom Faith Church is born.

1992 Space is required at the college, so Colin and Caroline Urquhart move to the Sussex town of Crawley, where the expanding Kingdom Faith Church will also relocate.

Kingdom Faith consists of an international speaking and teaching ministry, a Bible College and a church. A second college is at Lamplugh House in Yorkshire, while ex-students have begun similar courses in Leicester and several African countries.

Complementing Colin's ministry are other capable leaders with their own nationally recognised ministries; John McKay, the Bible College's Director of Studies, is a charismatic theologian. His pioneering Bible reading course, *The Way of the Spirit*, is a key part of the Kingdom Faith students' curriculum and has been adopted by many groups around Britain and overseas.

Michael Barling, the College Principal, is another national speaker who was in the forefront of the renewal movement; Nicholas Rivett-Carnac was the much loved vicar of St Mark's, Kennington, a well-known London church where renewal crossed over into corporate revival. More by accident than design, they are all ordained Anglicans. Pastoring the church is Dan Chesney, ordained in the American Four-Square movement; like Colin and John McKay he has produced books and teaching aids. Significantly, all have experienced some degree of revival amongst a body of believers, and all have been called to work alongside Colin.

In the midst of economic recession the ministry has grown substantially; the Sussex complex provides work for the sixty-five adults (some with families) who comprise the staff, or 'team' at Kingdom Faith. A Resources Centre mails books and tapes all over the world (Kingdom Faith Ministries is one of the largest Christian retailers in the country), with the result that 90 per cent of those who hear Colin's teaching will never see him in person. With all the other overheads which come with people, property and vehicles, Kingdom Faith needed approximately £15,000 a week to survive in 1992, although the team were unsalaried.

This national and international ministry fulfils a prophecy Colin received direct from God in 1970: 'Your voice will be heard amongst the nations. If you do not speak, my people will not hear.'

Yet by the early 1990s, Colin was declining most invitations to preach overseas, because God had told him to spend time doing the 'hidden' work which must be done if revival is to happen in the nation. He had to pray and prepare for revival.

The vision remains constantly with him: 'In my heart is a longing to see the purposes of God fulfilled and revival breaking out. But God wants us to break through *here* and then not only I but others will go out to the nations.'

Colin's preaching has a strong prophetic element.

For years he has preached without notes, ever since a daring experiment at St Thomas's, Letchworth, his second church. Realising he was spending too much time preparing sermons, he prepared for an evening service by spending extra time in prayer rather than writing notes. Once he stood up to preach, he found himself speaking biblical truths that were new even to him and receiving revelations seconds before his congregation. The evening congregation doubled after four weeks to eighty people and increased to one hundred and fifty within six months.

This dependence on God to speak through him lasted; his former assistant Guy Barton remembers that while Colin might have prepared for speaking engagements weeks in advance, on other occasions he went onto the platform not knowing what he would preach.

At other times his obedience was tested when he knew God had given him 'a real hornets' nest of a sermon' which would stir up trouble in the church which had invited him. Nonetheless, he learned that avoiding trouble by preaching on a safer topic would mean his words lost their anointing, the divine power to effect change in his listeners.

Since he believes that the easiest way to interpret Scripture is to believe it, most new listeners find it liberating to be able to take what God says at face value rather than apply a light mist of man's understanding. In the words of a new church member, used to shorter homilies, Roffey sermons are 'long, meaty and easy to understand'. As Colin knows that by teaching God's word he is presenting the truth, he encourages his listeners to respond because by doing so they will not only show they have understood his message, but by assenting they go some way towards receiving God's words as truth for their own lives. Frequently, if there is what he deems insufficient reaction from his listeners, he will challenge them with something like, 'Hello? Did I come to the right address? I mean, if I can understand this stuff, I'd have thought anyone could.' Usually his listeners giggle weakly and hastily mutter an 'Amen'. The convinced, those already on some sort of faith path, manage a 'Hallelujah'.

Marigold Pym, who was part of the ministry for several years, maintains that Colin is 'brilliant at making the word of God understandable. He makes it so simple, whereas people like theologians make it terribly complicated. He has this ability also to tie up scriptures from different places in the Bible which was just brilliant for us.'

Her husband Francis, an Anglican curate, was particularly attracted to his teaching on the Holy Spirit. 'Colin showed that the Holy Spirit is someone *in* you, rather than a part of God who is about somewhere.'

Both Francis and Marigold Pym found they retained teaching which had influenced not just their hearts but their minds through their understanding.

'What Colin did was to address our minds. It was as if he took hold of the mind of God and made these things perfectly straightforward and understandable and logical. Once we grasped them with our minds we received understanding, and the teaching wouldn't go away, because as Jesus said in the parable of the sower, it is those who hear the word and *understand* it who will retain it and produce a crop.' (Matthew 13:19–23)

Roffey Place

The Bible College at Roffey Place is a key part of the vision's outworking. (The story of the purchase of Roffey was an exercise in faith and is explained in chapter six.)

It was to be part of a revival centre, a concept which was born long before it came into existence. Housing a Bible College and later a church, its life and training were to evidence all the principles of personal and corporate revival that had been experienced at The Hyde.

'The Lord told us we would need a training college to train up people in ministries; not in denominational ministries, but that we would be sending out people with the fire of revival in their hearts', explains Colin.

When Colin, his family and a handful of close colleagues had gone in 1977 to The Hyde, a mansion set in several overgrown acres, they wondered what they were doing in a big country house. One woman, who had been fervently praying for a ministry base to be provided, took one look at its size and thought she had overdone the prayer. However, as they settled in, over a hundred people were called to join the newly-formed Bethany fellowship.

God also spoke to them prophetically about events that were to take place, including starting a training college. At the time they took that to mean that these would all happen at The Hyde, but during the course of time it became clear that The Hyde itself was going to be too small. One of the things God told them was that they would have a camp where people would come and meet with God. And since 1983 Kingdom Faith Ministries has held a camp at Newark and then Peterborough which has grown to accommodate nearly five thousand people every year; this could never have happened at The Hyde.

Colin himself moved into the house adjoining Roffey Place in May 1989, and took over the running of the college that September. His personal travelling ministry was gradually to become less onerous as he entered more fully into the life of the college over the next couple of years.

'An itinerant ministry only has validity if you are bringing God's prophetic word into the various situations you go into. For some years I'd been moving in that anointing, seeing whole situations open up because God used me to bring that prophetic word. A lot of healings and miracles would happen as confirmation of that. Wherever I went, I saw God's blessing as His Spirit moved in power.

'But it was like doing the donkey-work, just going round and seeing people breaking free into life and blessing and healing. Sometimes it was at big international conferences, at other times it was when visiting areas for local celebration meetings. But that blessing you see in those situations is some way short of revival. You can leave blessing behind you because people have been touched by God, but they don't go out with the dynamic of revival in their lives.'

As Colin began to speak and minister in Pentecostal churches, having known little about them before then, he found there was not the emphasis on the life of the Church, the body of Christ, and the commitment to one another. 'I began to see that although there were other churches coming alive then in the charismatic renewal, what God had been doing in Luton was even more gracious than I had realised at the time. If what was happening in other churches was described as renewal, what we had in Luton was revival. I mean, it was of a different order.'

This lifestyle, the practical outworking of the principles of revival Colin had learned over the years, was to be established both at Roffey and in everyone who went out from there. By now his teaching had been developed and refined by three major periods when he experienced God in dramatically new ways. As well as the revival period at Luton, where he saw the importance of love and unity amongst believers (explained further in Chapters Three and Four), there was a personal breakthrough into faith (described in Chapter Six) and the revival at The Hyde. All three stages now had to come together to be expressed in the life of Roffey.

So when Bob Gordon, an elder of the Bethany Fellowship and the college's first principal, moved to the Midlands and Colin had to take over as College Principal (he was already Director) he was able establish his revival ministry at Roffey Place. He arrived with his own personal team of twelve who had been with him in his Horsham offices. Only the Director of Studies John McKay and his wife Marguerite remained on the premises. Colin came in to virtually empty buildings and now had to establish the New Testament lifestyle with this group. Happily his first term had a full complement of students and numbers have steadily increased ever since then. As for the team, it expanded to sixty-five adults and their children in the next three years.

Amongst the Kingdom Faith team, Colin is regarded with a mixture of awe and affection. There is no pride in Colin's awareness of people's respect; God has wrought such changes in him over the years that he knows his character, like the rest of him, is no longer his own. Frequently during time away with the Lord, writing or on a ministry trip, God has dealt with him to effect what appear to him to be major changes in his outlook. He jokes about the changes, telephoning Caroline, his wife, before his return home to warn her to brace herself for yet another 'new' husband.

Despite the changes, Caroline maintains he is a simple man: 'He's a very stable person, not at all moody; he's humble, wanting only to serve and please God, and he openly confesses his sins. Of course he's changed since I first knew him, when he was very fearful and insecure, but God has dealt with that, making him bolder and bolder.'

According to Caroline, Colin is still getting used to the idea of a higher profile which God has led him to expect; it will be an unavoidable consequence of his desire to see the nation turned back to God.

The team's awe comes from their knowledge of the amount of time Colin spends on his own before God and the disciplined life which demands a stamina whose source can only be supernatural. Financial Manager Jim Penberthy, the longest-serving team member, says, 'Of all the well-known Christians I meet, I can honestly say that Colin's walk with the Lord is second to none.'

Happily Jim is one of those with the gift of administration, which Colin admits he does not have. Although acutely sensitive to the Holy Spirit's leading, both Colin's desk and daily schedule present a challenge to any time-management consultant.

His openness about his passions – Christ, cricket and coffee – an openness in itself difficult for a naturally shy man, and his jokes about his dislikes – criticism and correspondence – are some of the reasons for the team's affection. They see the unpretentious man behind the powerful preacher, the man who likes nothing better than a day at Lord's (better still, England winning at Lord's) and making rugs for his grandchildren's birthdays.

As one of his administrators said, after spending two days trying to track him down for a decision, 'Once you get into his study, he's such a dear you forget what you were cross about.' Another said, 'He's full of grace, so I can be completely honest with him.' In fact this same man was warned by his predecessor that the best way to get a decision from Colin was to present a fait accompli: 'If I don't hear otherwise, I'll spend two thousand pounds.' That usually got a swift answer.

Yet if Colin suddenly developed a liking for administration and replying to the many letters he receives, it would probably be at the expense of time with the Lord. As the 'eyes' of his ministry and church, the cost would be too great if he spent more time looking at the trees rather than the wood. Not that he is unaware of detail, however; most (perhaps too many) issues regarding the ministry's people and property are brought to him.

Colin's mastery of detail is revealed in his painting. Coming from an artistic family with an architect father, he could have been a professional painter and now teaches others how to paint when he occasionally has the time.

A recent work displayed in his office shows a woodland scene in pastels with a perspective that was not easy to achieve. In a foreground darkened by undergrowth and overbearing winter trees, a rickety, well-worn stile provides the sole access to a sunlit forest clearing. Apart from this unintended allusion to the Christian walk, such a painting could only be achieved by acute observation.

The observation extends to people as well. Absence from a meeting never goes unnoticed. One older team member wondered, half seriously, whether he had a bionic eye. Such things as unexplained absences are noticed but only commented on in general, without criticism directed in public to any individual. Although he impresses forcefully on the students that they have no right to choose what lectures to attend because God has called them to Roffey, he can show gentle concern on a one-to-one basis. A student summoned to his study after missing several meetings found he was simply concerned for her welfare. After a brief chat, he prayed for her.

For the small, close team who work for and travel with him, he always chooses 'encouragers', those with the gift of encouragement. This makes a lot of sense when one considers the opposition which he has endured. What is sad is that it often comes from those who may never have heard him speak – in my own experience I was baffled to hear his teaching on healing condemned on the strength of second-hand hearsay which, like Chinese whispers, was an untruth distorted by murmuring. His reaction is to forgive and get on with what God wants him to do. Taking the time to reply to wrong accusations can rob God of time He has designated for you to work for Him, and the longer you dwell on injustices, the more your own peace is disturbed. Far better to listen to God and continue doing constructive work for His Kingdom.

It is equally surprising to hear how even a straightforward teacher like Colin can be misunderstood at first hand. Sadly, people can sometimes misunderstand because they feel that what has been said does not tally with their own experience, especially when their experience is weighing heavily on them. An example of this occurred recently when Colin talked about his work on counselling and his opposition to pseudo-psychological methods used by some sections of the Church to deal with people's past problems. Immediately afterwards he received a note challenging his supposed assertion that people should not deal with problems gathered in their past. This was a typical misunderstanding; Colin was telling his audience that all such problems should be brought to the cross and the sufferer should be encouraged to concentrate on the truth of their new identity in Christ rather than their old identity as a victim of circumstances.

Counselling is only part of the ministry to train and encourage God's people. The real mission is to get them ready for revival, and there is no danger of God letting him forget it. Reminders come in personal prayer and in public. A typical one came on 6th May 1992 during his personal prayer time, which he felt appropriate to share with the resident team:

'Keep the vision clear and do not diminish it. Pray it into being. I will only increase a vision.'

Later, during the worship time, he brought the following prophecy which echoed an earlier, longer one he had received on 24th February 1992:

'Have I not said that mountains will be levelled and valleys raised?

'Am I not the Lord who changes things to such an

extent? I and I alone can do this. Am I not able to do everything I have promised? Men make promises often when they are unable to keep them. I can never do that because My ability is without limit.

'No matter what I promise, I am able to deliver it. Every promise I have made to you personally I will carry out. As you trust in Me and believe My word, so will I put that promise into effect in your life.

'So rejoice in that and walk in the certain knowledge that I will do what I have promised.'

Following God's vision requires total commitment. There is no room for anyone in the ministry who does not share it. This is as true for a young person serving God in the kitchen as it is for the leaders. Often Colin has been led to take certain people under his wing by inviting them to join his personal team, because God wants them to learn from him, even though to others it has not been apparent. 'In the end I see why Colin's taken them on, and what God had wanted to do for them, but at the beginning you can wonder why God's picked that person,' said Caroline. 'I don't have anywhere near the same relationship with God as Colin, but as Colin says, if I had, I'd be him! And very seldom has Colin made a mistake in selecting someone.'

One notable occasion when it seemed as if a mistake had been made concerned Guy Barton, who was to become a successful assistant for Colin before going on to work for another church. After a three-month trial period, it was clear to both Guy and Colin that theirs was not a relationship made in heaven. Neither was a natural ice-breaker; both were cautious and taciturn. As Guy was also living in Colin's house at the time, he found himself exhausted by emotional undercurrents; if he sat down in the sitting-room, how would he know if he was in Colin's chair? Prepared to throw in the towel and admit that he had mistaken God's call to work for Colin, he came down to breakfast one day to discover that the Holy Spirit had broken the ice. From then on he liked Colin enormously and they were to derive pleasure from talking about ordinary, 'unspiritual' things. It also helped that he liked cricket.

While Colin has been used to build up other people's ministries, those with other God-given visions have usually recognised that they will not be comfortable if, even half-consciously, their spirit is urging them in another direction. Men like Charles Sibthorpe and Bob Gordon were mightily used by God during their years as elders of the Bethany Fellowship based at The Hyde, and their personal ministries blossomed under Colin's leadership. In time, however, they recognised that God had given them different visions and they went on to new work of their own. Charles has a thriving church and a travelling ministry, while Bob's vision for evangelism (he started the King's Coaches) is being fulfilled at his own centres for training and outreach. Splits are painful, but an arrow with a divided shaft has difficulty flying and misses its target.

Thus Colin's vision has been through fire. If his ministry is seen as the tip of an arrow, then that tip is now made of tempered steel. There has been opposition, which on one or two occasions could have had a devastating effect on the ministry. Doubly hurtful had been the fact that it came from those he regarded as personal friends, apparently united in their concept of service to God. But through these experiences Colin's obedience to God and to the vision for revival have been tested. A warning he received many years ago from an older, more experienced minister has helped bolster him against the effects of criticism:

'Never,' he was told, 'accept criticism from anyone whose ministry is less fruitful than yours.'

In fact his most satisfying relationships with leaders in recent years have been forged with men from overseas who have the same vision for their own countries. He has known Harry Westcott of Canberra, Australia for sixteen years and often ministered in his church while Harry has led seminars for Colin, imbuing them with his own florid expressions such as, 'Why do we try to cut costs where God's concerned? He's El Shaddai, not El Cheapo!'

Then there is Ulf Ekman from Uppsala, Sweden, about whom Colin says, 'God knit our hearts together.' Ulf's vision for Sweden is similar to Colin's vision for Britain, although in practice Ulf's methods and style have been different. His Word of Life Church has established a Bible School, a Christian primary and high school, and a Christian university.

With the collapse of the Iron Curtain, an event some other friends of Colin's at cental Germany's Glaubenszentrum (Faith Centre) had been praying for, Word of Life church members hired a train to carry the gospel message throughout the former USSR. They have planted scores of new churches in Scandinavia, Russia and Eastern Europe. Word of Life members have also been active in helping Soviet Jews emigrate to Israel, recognising their biblical obligation to bless God's chosen people.

Unstinting obedience to God's slightest instructions is the key to this ministry's success. When a colleague asked God why Ulf should be so greatly blessed, the Holy Spirit replied, 'Because if I told him to put a fifth tyre on his car, he'd do it for Me'.

At the annual Eurofire conference in 1987, organised by Christ For All Nations (the ministry of Reinhard Bonnke), Colin heard Ray McCauley of Randburg, South Africa. A former bodybuilder and a Mr Universe finalist, Ray leads the sixteen-thousand-strong Rhema Church with over six hundred other 'planted' churches. In South Africa he is nationally known because his gospel preaching brings together all races while at the same time he has warned against the possible persecution of Christians which could result if an embittered black majority voted for a Communist government in that country.

Both Ulf Ekman and Ray McCauley delivered what Colin considered to be 'strategic, prophetic messages into the life of Britain'; both men have also prophesied about Colin's future as a spiritual leader.

Ray believes big churches will develop, especially in London, where it would be quite feasible to see a church of fifty thousand. Large churches have already developed in those parts of the world seeing revival, such as Korea, South America and China. Prophecies from others, confirmed by God's personal words to him, led

Colin to believe that he too would pastor a 'mega-church'.

Kingdom Faith Church

From The Hyde period onwards, there was pressure to start a church. The ministry was dedicated to going out into all the world, but that did not prevent people with damaging problems seeking healing at The Hyde. There was no doubt they needed looking after, but who was to do it? In addition certain local people wanted to worship with the community at The Hyde, so a fellowship grew up around the ministry and eventually moved to Roffey Place.

However, after creating the Bible College at Roffey, it was believed that God wanted to put the next piece of the jigsaw in its rightful place. To be a proper revival centre which reached out to its surroundings on several levels, there had to be the college, a resources centre for literature and tapes, and a church. But not just a cosy 'bless me' club. The church had to be a model church, a revived church whose members were leading New Testament lives.

When Colin met Dan Chesney, an American evangelist and pastor whom God had called to England, the similarity of their vision was striking. It was no coincidence that Dan had also had the words 'revival centre' impressed on his mind by the Holy Spirit, nor that he had experienced revival both personally and in his church. Both men recognised that their spiritual and personal affinity was God's doing. Colin invited Dan to speak at Faith camps and then to help launch and pastor Kingdom Faith Church. Dan knew the work was the fulfilment of part of his call to England and despite his abilities as a preacher and evangelist he was keen to be discipled by Colin.

The church grew rapidly, from seventy to four hundred in just eight months. This was what the Lord led Colin to expect – a church of thousands.

'Numbers aren't everything but if God says, "Build a big church", then numbers must be significant,' he says.

Perhaps the growth is not surprising, considering that the sermon quality would be suitable for a full-blown conference and the music is exceptional. Colin and Dan hope that people are attracted to the church by its vision, however, which is unashamedly for revival. Its members commit themselves to pray for the church and its vision. In their Bibles they carry a card:

> A people living in the revival power of Jesus Christ their Lord;
> Committed to a life of faith in God's word;
> Laying down their lives one for another in love;
> And revealing His light and truth to the world.

Kingdom Faith Church, born in 1992, is now up and running with the revival flame lit in the early 1970s and rekindled in the early 1980s at The Hyde. The ten-month period of revival blessing at The Hyde, was, Colin was told, a supernatural act of God's grace. Not that the community was passive in this process; they were praying for up to six hours a day and earnestly seeking God's face; it was simply that the depth of God's presence and power of His works were far out of proportion to the human input, as in previously chronicled revivals. The revival power at The Hyde gradually diminished, although the ministry had attracted many in that time. The ministry team had grown to over a hundred people, and therein lay the seeds of the revival's demise. Sadly, not everyone who joined brought the same revival dynamic with them, as they had not experienced it, so compromise crept in and the strength of faith for revival was watered down.

Some consolation came through the revelation that although in future everyone would have to persevere more in seeking God, the ministry would be at the heart of the next revival. And Colin and his team now knew the difference between revival and renewal, which was what the ministry lived in from 1983 to 1992. The powerful preaching, the healings, changed lives and miracles of God's provision continued as outward signs of His blessing on the work, but no-one could have persuaded them that they were still in revival. Yet the experience had taught Colin how to bring people into personal revival in readiness for a corporate move of the Holy Spirit. He now understood all the ingredients which needed to be distilled for 'God's people to live in the fullness of His truth'.

Throughout this period Colin continued to write books, speak to churches all over the country and teach students at the Training Centre. Life was certainly busy, but he knew that all this activity was preparation for 'the big one'.

The next time of revival would be the last time: 'We'd get into it and stay in it,' was how one of Colin's team put it. 'It's for the rest of our lifetime,' said another, 'so we have to know how to stay in that place with God.'

Yet revival is only bestowed by God on those whom he can trust to bring it to others. 'Revival isn't a nice piece of blessing,' asserts Colin. 'It's meeting with God in such a way that a revolution takes place in your life.'

Those who have tasted revival are not satisfied with anything less and continue praying for it. It leaves bitter sweet memories with those who have experienced its joy – and a determination to see it repeated in their lifetime.

Former Kingdom Faith students remember times when God seemed especially close to the whole college. Guy Barton recalls two periods when he 'would not even consider sinning'. At night he would be woken up and found himself praying – 'I couldn't do anything else.' When he looked out of his window, he saw lights on in students' bedrooms all round the building. Director of Studies John McKay talks of 'visitations', times when Jesus seemed to be walking the corridors and people hardly dared raise their voices.

Several of the people still working for Kingdom Faith Ministries experienced God's revival power at The Hyde or in other churches. For all of them, their experience of God's presence at that time had an intensity they will never forget, which has bonded them to the ministry.

Before being called to the college, John McKay and his wife Marguerite ministered in three churches over a period of ten years. In each one they saw God's reviving power at work as a result of a group of people being obedient to God's call. Marguerite's face still lights up at the memory:

'When you're in revival, you're very conscious of Jesus' presence and His love all the time. He's simply there, right at the centre of the work. You feel as if it's forever and is never going to end.'

Annette Callaway was just seventeen when God's presence swept into The Hyde. Seeing God work miraculously in people increased her faith so that she could trust God with those areas of her life where faith had been lacking previously.

'I'd seen Him, I'd felt Him and I'd touched Him. Once you've met with God like that, the hunger is to have it again and not just for a little while, but to live in it.'

Typically of those who have experienced something of revival, even though only in a local setting, Annette still struggles to understand how to stay in personal revival. In her eyes she has failed to some extent because she is no longer enjoying the same closeness to God. 'I have to do so many more things in my own strength again. I know I could be much more Spirit-led, doing things the way God wants rather than trying to work them out myself.'

With her evangelist husband Kevin and young son, Annette returned from America to rejoin Kingdom Faith in 1992. After working with YWAM (Youth With A Mission) in sunny California, they believed it right to seek God in West Sussex. Kevin became the new church's Director of Evangelism and one of the college lecturers, which gave full scope for his interest in evangelism through the performing arts. Like others who were led to join the new church, including a couple called from Ray McCauley's church in South Africa, they had the word 'revival' impressed on their hearts.

When Kevin and Annette arrived back in June 1992, they were in time to hear Colin speak a prophecy which could have been interpreted as a signpost for their futures:

'There is coming a time of great travail and turmoil on the earth. But those who know how to stand, will stand and shine. Those who will stand are those who learn to be humble in My sanctuary. Many who refuse to listen to My word will turn.

'Beloved, I need a people of My own, a people for Myself, who will not be shaken by the turmoil. I call *you* to be such a people. If you are such a people, you will have nothing to fear. It will seem as if the events around you cannot touch you, such will be My protection for those who trust Me. They will not affect you; I will surround you. I am preparing a people to stand firm. Do not seek to go off in independence in your own ways in the time of shaking, but stand *together*.

'Do not give the evil one any opportunity to rejoice over you. He wants to separate and divide you. Those in independence and isolation can easily be separated. Do not allow him to deceive you. Stand together and test every spirit to see that it is of God. Have I not said that nations will be shaken? Men do not understand how this will happen, nor the swiftness with which it will take place. This is why My children must be ready.

'Beloved, this is no time to be concerned with trivial things or superficial issues. This is a time to walk in My ways, to walk together and not to let anything distract you from the walk of faith which I have planned for you.'

These words are typical of many heard in recent years, although Colin is all too aware of the imperfection of prophetic utterances by humans. Nor can such long-range forecasts even be adequately tested until they come to pass. As the apostle Paul said, 'We know in part and prophesy in part.' (1 Corinthians 13:9)

Like other, similar prophecies, this message implies that judgement and persecution are not far away, with which Colin concurs while pointing to God's graciousness.

'Of course the nation deserves judgement – every nation does – but God's judgement is tempered by mercy. And in His grace God will visit Britain.'

When revival comes, the nation's spiritual ethos will change, with a move back to God and the Bible. Opposition will also come from those whose iniquity has been unchecked, such as those involved in vice and drugs. God's people will have so much spiritual power, however, that wickedness will be overcome. Thus Colin believes talking about death and destruction, without including the good news of all God has provided through Christ, is not true to Scripture.

Most of his life has been lived in an attempt to obey God's call to prepare His people for revival, helping others discover the holiness and majesty of God, the joy of knowing Jesus and empowerment by the Holy Spirit. If judgement is on the way, he sees no need to over-emphasise it in his teaching and insists, 'There are so many prophets of doom around that I feel the Lord wants to emphasise the positive. Even in Scripture there are prophecies of judgement, but there's always hope as well. God promises that if the nation repents, then He will pour out His riches and His blessings. And I believe the prophetic word of God is not so much that there is judgement on the way, but there's revival on the way. God isn't prophesying death and destruction on the nation – quite the opposite.

'This is where the whole business of grace comes in; it really is the mystery of God. You could say it's because Britain has given missionaries to the rest of the world that God is going to measure back blessing. Britain has had a strategic place with its lines of communication going all over the world. It once had an empire – now its spiritual empire will change not only Europe but reach as far as the United States.'

Nonetheless, Colin believes that revival in itself will bring a kind of judgement between those who are moving with God and those who are not. He quotes the scripture that certain people will be saved, 'but only as one escaping through the flames'. (1 Corinthians 3:15)

In other words, fire will test what we are building in our lives. 'God is calling His people back all the time. You can face issues in your life or ignore them. If you face them, you come into a closer walk with Jesus.'

One of the watchwords for Britain today is as true today as it was in the time of the prophet Isaiah:

> 'I live in a high and holy place,
> but also with him who is contrite and lowly
> in spirit,

> to revive the spirit of the lowly
> and to revive the heart of the contrite.' (Isaiah 57:15)

Revival follows on very closely from our own personal walk with God, which must be one of holiness. The individual must walk in righteousness, submission, obedience and love. As these qualities mark the individual's dealings with others, so God will bring His sovereign revival into that particular situation.

But there is no conquest without conflict. Colin and others discovered that the well-known expression, 'Revival will cost you everything' is too true to be dismissed as hyperbole. 'It's no good saying nice prayers, "O do come and revive us, Lord"; God is telling us to keep pressing in with Him so we're in a position to receive all He has for us.'

Thus personal revival is bringing individuals into a walk with Jesus where they obey Him: 'If you obey my commands, you will remain in my love, just as I have obeyed my Father's commands and remain in his love.' (John 15:10)

The cost begins with us personally. As Annette Callaway said, 'You can't make revival happen, but you can make yourself absolutely available. We have to ask ourselves whether we're willing for what revival's going to mean to us personally. God desires to bring revival to the whole nation – I have no doubt about that – but unless individuals are willing to pay the price it won't happen.'

Having experienced God's power being poured out on a group of people, she had the blessings but also knew the cost of reaching that place with God. 'Most of us just want the nice side, and think of all the blessings people receive, but unless you stop to find out what revival really is, you don't realise the cost of getting there and staying there.'

Revival is on God's agenda – but is it on ours? Those who want to change the nation have to start by letting God change them. Personal revival is essential if we are to see local and national revival. This book will show how people can change and have changed when they have come face to face with the vision for revival. The vision may be exclusive, but only in terms of demanding everything from those called to bring revival into being. It does not belong exclusively to Colin Urquhart but to the thousands of men and women in Britain and other countries who want to see God's purposes fulfilled.

And when the vision becomes the reality? That's when those who are prepared come into their own. The fact that this book draws on examples of lives changed by one ministry should not exclude anyone else from seeking God for themselves in readiness for His next sovereign move. The teaching comes from God, so to Him be the glory.

John McKay tells new Bible College students, 'When God moves, it's important to be ready.' Colin Urquhart would add that God will not move until we are ready. That's what this book is about.

Chapter Two

KNOWING GOD'S CALL

'If God has a call on your life, nothing, but nothing will stop it', says Colin Urquhart. 'The purpose of your new birth is to enable you to follow Jesus – that's the call of every Christian. This entails more than wandering to the front of a meeting and making a commitment. It involves repenting and *leaving the past behind*. Then you're free to follow Jesus and obey His call on your life.'

In fact it was a revelation for Colin that God would still fulfil His purposes in his life even if Colin made mistakes. From 1970 to May 1990 he lived with an 'awesome sense of responsibility' because of the calling God had given him. Would he miss it? God released him from his sense of impending failure with two words: 'You can't'. Even mistakes would work for the good of him who loved God and was called according to His purpose. (Romans 8:28)

Love is a key here; it reassures us that God leads His sheep.

'Love won't leave you dangling on the end of a string not knowing what direction to take,' Colin says.

What if a Christian is desperately praying for guidance but hears nothing? John McKay has a straightforward solution: 'God's waiting for you to do the last thing He told you to do!'

Scripture shows that our future is predestined, but God will never remove our free will; the Holy Spirit working in us will bring us to the destiny He has for each of us.

'For the Lord Almighty has purposed, and who can thwart him?' (Isaiah 14:27)

Colin explains this paradox by saying, 'God decided that you would decide!'

In his experience, people confuse reward and

inheritance. Many rewards are for now; as we reap what we sow, we receive back the measure we have given (one of Colin's favourite Kingdom principles). Some people strive in their Christian walk, fearing that they will lose their inheritance, whereas if they understood how much God loved them they would want to love Him back. 'You don't go soaring off into rebellion because you don't want to miss Him,' Colin explains.

One reason Colin gives for apparently traumatic events is that we may have to be stopped in our tracks after going in the wrong direction. He uses the example of Peter denying Jesus in Gethsemane but being restored to his Lord after bitter repentance.

'Jesus doesn't monkey around with us when we make wrong decisions', explains Colin. 'When you make wrong decisions you go backwards, not forwards. But in order to restore you to Himself, Jesus needs you to repent so you can get back on course. That's why He asked Peter if he loved Him more than his fishing and worldly occupations. (John 21:15) Once Peter laid down his old life again, he could be forgiven and prepared to enter the destiny planned for him before the beginning of the world.'

It is clear from the Bible that God has a plan for each one of us. In Acts 17:26 Paul says:

> 'From one man he made every nation of men, that they should inhabit the whole earth; and he determined the times set for them and the exact places where they should live. God did this so that men would seek him and perhaps reach out for him and find him, though he is not far from each one of us.'

In the Psalms we read: 'I cry out to God Most High, to God who fulfils his purpose for me.' (Psalm 57:2)

And He goes further than just determining where we should live; once our lives are surrendered to His gracious care we are able to tread the path He has ordained for us.

For Colin the key to knowing one's call lies in one word: submission. Churches and leaders must submit every area of activity completely to God's authority; individual members of churches must submit to their leaders whom God has placed over them. He is not impressed by those who believe they need bow to no earthly authority; the body of Christ was meant to be interdependent. 'If anyone thinks he can go it alone, he's a one-man church', he warns.

It is the surrender of one's 'free' will which is the stumbling block for many Christians; yet unless one is completely yielded to God, it is unlikely one will be able to determine and fulfil one's call in the way He intends.

Colin sums up the apparent paradox of active surrender:

'God has a purpose for you, but *He*, not you, will fulfil it. This does *not* mean that we can sit back passively, waiting for God to move the mountains. No, Jesus says clearly that we must take up our cross and *follow* Him. He will put before us the things we must do and *we* have to do them!'

Some words which impressed themselves particularly on Colin were those which Job spoke to God: 'I know that you can do all things; no plan of yours can be thwarted.' (Job 42:2)

God's plans include His plan for our lives; obviously we need to know His plan so we can test our daily activities against it. 'God wants you to know where you are going – both short term and long term. Walking in faith is *not* walking in blindness – it is knowing your goal! So whether you have had words spoken prophetically to your heart by God or words spoken about your life by someone else, you need to pray them into being', Colin explains.

In fact Dan Chesney believes Satan has deceived Christians about the concept of waiting on the Lord. 'It's not sitting around being passive – it means you're doing all you can while expecting God to move. Satan's strategy takes various forms, but he's fondest of giving you excuses about why you shouldn't get on with what God's told you to do. He'll suggest to people who have been Christians for fifty years that it's not now the *time* to do anything. Or he'll say you need more training to witness for Jesus. And surely you'll need more confirmation – like a thousand words of knowledge, then a sign, then a fleece!'

Colin used the illustration of a rug he had been making to show how God views our path to the fulfilment of His plans for us. Although the pleasant pattern on the rug was almost completed, one's eye was immediately drawn to a bare patch in one corner, which represented a particularly complicated section of the pattern. In its unfinished state, the rug was useless – it would probably trip you up! So it is with our personal progress; God has a path for us to follow and if we try to by-pass the parts which seem less pleasant or easy, He will simply bring us back to that part until His pattern has been completed.

'Of course', said Colin, 'if, when you eventually reach one of your life's goals, it seems you have come a circuitous route by the back doubles, guess whose fault that is? It's certainly not God's fault!'

Hearing God's voice

Receiving guidance (in words rather than pictures) from God, can be narrowed down to three sources:

– From the *rhema* word, the Greek term signifying 'the word for the moment'; usually a sentence or passage becomes 'highlighted' in your mind when you are reading the Bible.

– The instruction of God's Spirit to your spirit; often it is tempting to think you are just making up things when you seem to speak to yourself. In case of doubt, tell every other voice but that of the Holy Spirit to be quiet! If praying in tongues, ask God for the interpretation.

– Direct instruction from God. You can tell it is God because He tends to cut across whatever else you are praying about. This may not happen more than two or three times in a lifetime.

Learning to discern God's voice is one of the main aims of a Kingdom Faith student's course. One young man, 'Richard', who worked at Roffey, used to hear God speak quite clearly about important events in his life; he was told when he would get married (before he met the girl) and when he would go to theological college. At the interview for a place at the college, he was put in a group with three others. They were told to say things to the others which would bless them. The others spoke a few comforting scriptures. Richard tuned in to the Holy Spirit and produced three words of knowledge which encouraged each in their situation and contained information he could not possibly have known naturally.

'Words of knowledge' about other people's futures are, however, treated with caution at Kingdom Faith, especially when they concern jobs and potential marriage partners. Students and church members are encouraged to share their messages with the leadership so their accuracy can be 'tested' before revealing them to those concerned.

Testing what people believe God is saying to them will become increasingly important, just as the Bible warns (Matthew 24:24), believes Michael Barling. 'I get a bit cynical because I have people coming into my office saying God's told them to marry so-and-so. Ten weeks later, they've been told to do something completely different. If I had a tenth of the instruction from God that some people have, I'd be very happy!'

Elizabeth Allan, who was to give up a career as a research scientist to join the Kingdom Faith team, was taught a lesson about the futility of adding her own interpretation to God's words. In 1988 God had asked her out of the blue, 'Are you prepared to go to prison for me?' She started imagining the modern-day equivalent of being thrown to the lions and gulped as she replied, 'Yes, Lord, if it's you I'm going to prison for.'

After that step of obedience God revealed her call to her, that of full-time intercession. Since nothing more was said about prison, Elizabeth assumed that she would be thrown into prison as some consequence of her call to be an intercessor! For three years God was silent on the subject of prison until He began to point out to her that all He had said was, 'Are you prepared to go to prison for me?' not 'Are you prepared to be thrown into prison?' He began to reveal to her that it was prison work He was speaking about rather than languishing in some dark, foreign jail.

'That was a lesson to me in paying attention to the *exact words* that God uses.'

Gradually, the call became clearer, but a wait was involved. Four years after God's original question, the door to Holloway swung open. 'A friend heard that women were being sought who were called by God to visit Holloway Prison's medical wing,' recalls Elizabeth. 'At the same time I read a report by a woman who had gone for a preliminary visit to the psychiatric and drug addict wings. She had been so affected and distressed by what she saw that she had been unable to sleep that night. When I heard this, I felt my gut being wrenched in an agonising identification with the women who were in such appalling misery. For the next week, every time I thought of it, I broke down in tears. I knew that God was calling me to this work and He confirmed it at the same time through many scriptures. For instance, He told me to read Matthew 25:36. Not knowing what was in that scripture, I looked it up and read, "I was in prison and you visited me."'

Hearing from God can of course be fun. Often one senses He is inviting us to laugh at our own unbelief, especially when a scripture or Bible reference containing a reminder to be thankful drops into one's mind at a negative moment! One amusing example perfectly illustrated God's grace and wit to me. At the end of a teaching day held by Dan Chesney for the church's Certificate in Ministry course, he invited people to come forward for prayer to have their call confirmed or their anointing revealed. I went forward, rather idly thinking it would be nice to hear something specific from the Lord. All around me, people were receiving prophecies and falling over under the power of the Holy Spirit. For me – nothing. Next day, Sunday, I took part in Faith Factory, the children's sessions where Colin and Dan believe God will bring a revival like Colin saw in his ministry in Luton. The emphasis is very much on teaching children to rely on God's word for themselves as they develop a relationship with Jesus through reading the Bible and prayer. It is also hoped that they will be able to practise using the gifts of the Holy Spirit in a safe environment where they need not feel self-conscious. Children who come to Faith Factory are encouraged to ask Jesus into their lives if they have not already done so and usually receive the baptism of the Holy Spirit and the gift of tongues shortly afterwards.

At the end of that morning's activities Peter Hellyer, the director of children's work, invited them to pray in tongues and ask God to show them someone present to whom they were to give some words from Him. Next they were to pray and ask God for the message.

No sooner had I finished praying than I saw six-year-old Vicky in front of me, grinning toothily. For about three minutes she related certain things to me which assured me of how closely God was watching everything I did, including a confirmation that I was to work in Faith Factory with the children. Two questions I had had on my mind were answered. I was also wondering about my activities for the rest of that day. Quite suddenly Vicky wagged a finger at me and warned, 'Don't drive. Stay in and relax in the Lord.' She could not possibly have known that I was wondering whether to go out to lunch which involved a fairly long drive.

When she had finished, I tried to write down some of the words. But when I asked Vicky to recap something, she had reverted to being an ordinary six-year-old and was demonstrating how to stand on one leg for thirty seconds!

'What was that bit about?' I asked, scribbling furiously.

'Twenty-six, twenty-seven . . .' intoned Vicky.

I dined out on the story for a week.

She was followed by an eleven-year-old boy who spoke for less time but told me about my recent past in much more sophisticated language than he normally used and told me about something for which God wanted me to receive prayer. He was happy to do the honours.

Later a nine-year-old girl came and gave me the words of Psalm 23, which conveyed just as much for my circumstances as the others had.

Again, I was comforted and amazed at God's concern for details of my life and His humour at my expense in using 'the mouths of babes' to pour out His Holy Spirit. Indeed, it is widely believed that the coming revival will see a move of God amongst young people who will be used in supernatural ways that the previous generation could not imagine.

The call to study

There is no typical call to a Kingdom Faith course, although taking time off to study usually precipitates some sort of disruption in prospective students' lives. Often older students have given up their secular jobs and sold their houses to raise the fees. As one married woman, who was called to Roffey from Australia, said, 'If God wants you at Roffey, He'll get you there.'

Some come because they have received a good report of the course; some hear God speaking to them very directly about coming. 'In every case the call was fairly well tested', remembers Guy Barton, Colin's former assistant, 'in that not only the applicant but also the leadership needed to hear that God was calling that particular person. Mistakes were made, as you would expect – some people came and found it wasn't the right place or it was all too much for them, or they didn't like what was happening to them there and couldn't or wouldn't work through the implications of it in their lives. But for the vast majority it was absolutely the right place and you saw people changing, which was wonderful to watch.'

Guy himself had met someone who had been at Roffey and told him about his time there, then shortly afterwards he went to hear Colin preaching at Blackpool. 'I was tremendously struck by the ministry that he and the team had. From that point onwards I wanted to go on one of the leaders' weeks that were taking place at The Hyde. I never managed to get to one of those, but some time later the Lord made it clear to me that I was to go to Roffey to do one of the training courses.'

Guy claims to have 'pestered' the Lord for a long time to do theological training but was always refused until he asked about studying at Roffey. This call was also confirmed by his pastor at home.

The interview was a fairly typical one for a prospective

student who clearly has a call to come to study – it was concluded in five minutes. Guy saw Michael Barling who asked him why he thought he should come. Guy explained why and Michael simply said, 'I think you should come, too.'

John McKay warns students who go to see Colin, 'You'll go in to see a man who looks at you absolutely deadpan because he's got one ear out for the Lord!'

Colin recalls that it was pointless to interview certain students:

'They would come into my study and I discerned at once in my spirit that not only would they stay for more than one term but they'd go on to join the team!'

This was the case with Guy, who heard from God halfway through his time at Roffey that he was not to return home to Cumbria, as he had expected, but that he would be working alongside someone in an apostolic ministry. He immediately started looking round the country for someone with an apostolic ministry. It was about two months later that God put into his mind the idea of working with Colin. Happily Colin also expressed interest in Guy joining his team.

'When I went to see Colin he asked some pretty deep questions, but he is very gentle. He'll give you time to think and mull over what he's said before he expects an answer. Similarly he won't always say what's on his own mind, but will pray about it before coming out with what he was thinking.'

Colin's stillness and careful use of words can unnerve those unused to him; although he has a dry sense of humour, ('Sometimes even Caroline doesn't know when I'm serious!') he also has a finely-tuned awareness of what Roffey pastor Nicholas Rivett-Carnac calls 'the Holy Spirit's time economy'. Nicholas believes a turning point for Colin came when he discovered he actually *could* accomplish all he had to do each day.

Hence Colin's intent expression which discourages small talk. Leading by example as ever, he expects his team to develop the same respect for the value of time; revival begins, he says, when you realise your time is not your own. An edict issued to the new Kingdom

Faith Church's life (house) groups stated briskly that '7.30–9.00 p.m. is for serious study, not chit-chat.' Coffee and chit-chat were allowed from 9.00–9.30 p.m.

Guy knew he was in the presence of a godly man.

'I had, and still have, tremendous respect for Colin. Of course, since I got to know him over five years, I realised that he's actually a very ordinary person in himself – and yet a very godly person. That's in evidence when he's speaking on the platform; he comes across as a real man of God who brings forth the word of God with authority. Then he steps down from the platform to mingle with the crowd and suddenly he's just a completely ordinary person relating to people in perfectly ordinary ways. That always astonished me – still does, I guess.'

More leaders like Guy are now being encouraged to apply to Kingdom Faith Bible College for one- or two-year training courses. Yet even those who believe they are called to full-time ministry will probably find God has more in store than they expected.

In one of his opening addresses to new students, John McKay quoted Psalm 43:3–4:

> 'Send forth your light and your truth,
> let them guide me;
> let them bring me to your holy mountain,
> to the place where you dwell.
> Then will I go to the altar of God,
> to God, my joy and my delight.
> I will praise you with the harp,
> O God, my God.'

He told the students, 'God's light has brought us to Roffey to be guided by His truth. Once here we go to the altar, which involves both worship and *sacrifice.* Here we sacrifice all that God asks us to lay down – everything that might have given us status in the world. Some of us have already made sacrifices – we've given up jobs, homes, worldly status.

'At some point in every term, after enjoying the relief of not having to cook and go to an office, say, for nine weeks, certain students suddenly realise they have lost their previous identity and feel uncomfortable at the lack of status. Now it's just you – and God – at the altar; it's a lonely place.

'But this is where God will bless you so that you can bless others and minister more powerfully than before. The more you lay aside, the more God comes in and fills you. He wants 100% of you, not 50%, 60% or even 95%! Once you give Him 100% of yourself, you are in a position to receive all of your inheritance as a child of God.'

When people are totally committed to God, things often move fast. Thus the pace of life at Roffey can be hectic, in particular the pace of change. Guy Barton explains: 'At Roffey you've got about fifty staff who are totally committed to the Lord, all of whom to varying degrees are listening to the Lord, wanting to hear what He is saying. So as soon as the Lord reveals His vision, whether it's through Colin or corporately, people want to follow that. Now obviously they have to work through the challenges that come with any vision, but because they're so committed to the Lord it doesn't take too long.'

Like any college students, Roffey students want to know where to go next. Unlike university students, they need to know exactly where *God* wants them to work. Towards the end of term, pressure (mainly in one's own mind) increases if there is no clear call either to move on somewhere specific or stay and join the Kingdom Faith team. For this reason being a student at Roffey can be spiritually exhausting as the individual, alongside tens of others, seeks God's will.

No-one should underestimate the effect of unaccustomed spiritual activity. Many Christians have experienced meetings and Christian 'holidays' where they have been changed by an unusually profound experience of God. While they will benefit enormously in the long term, there has often been a spiritual upheaval to which they need to accustom themselves in the short term.

The atmosphere at Roffey is both peaceful and dynamic, but even those used to full-time ministry discover that living in this atmosphere is initially taxing. Guy Barton now manages the Community Centre of a fast-growing church in Southampton. Yet he finds the pace slower now, despite the fact that he and his colleagues believe their church will be used significantly in reviving the Christian life of the area.

John McKay tells new students, 'You must expect to change here. You'll learn about history, the Bible and doctrine, but the main thing is that you'll change.'

Duncan Shearing, a student from Suffolk who later teamed up with Humphrey, a surveyor from Surrey, to start a revival ministry in Suffolk, said after his first term of intense spiritual progress: 'When I got home, everyone seemed to be going at a slower pace. I had a new power within me and wanted to share it. No-one seemed to want to speed up, though, because they hadn't received what I had.'

Testifying to the amount he had changed through making a concentrated effort to follow God for ten weeks, another student said, 'You might as well change your name at the end of term, because you'll be a different person.'

Hence there is a dynamic at Kingdom Faith that you would not find in a normal church, believes Guy Barton. 'In my church now we have as many church meetings as Kingdom Faith, but they're geared to the ordinary person in the street, whereas the meetings at Roffey assume that people are really wanting to follow the Lord and are available and able to give a great deal of time to the Lord. So things tend to happen at a somewhat greater pace and greater depth at Roffey.'

Guy himself changed a great deal during his time at Roffey. As an assistant pastor he had looked upon himself as a pastor and leader; he was used to co-pastoring a church, leading a youth group and working with evangelistic teams. Although he had come from a position where he felt he had a closely defined ministry, he realised quite soon after his arrival at Roffey that he would have to lay down that ministry.

'One of the things I used to do was to hide behind my ministry,' he explains. 'I presented a façade to people that said, "This is a leader", but not a great deal of my own character would come out. I knew my weaknesses and I wasn't prepared to display them; it was deception on my part to display an image and not to be vulnerable to other people.'

Very soon after coming to Roffey, Guy knew he would have to be vulnerable if he was to grow. 'I had to become real with people, so they could relate to the real me and not the façade to which I had wanted them to relate.'

As John McKay asked the new students, 'Why hold on to pride or status? Things that the world gives can be taken away, whereas things that God gives will simply improve year by year. What God gives you is forever and doesn't wear out.'

John used the example of the Israelites following God to show the students and team whether they were in the place God wanted them to be:

> 'On the day the tabernacle, the Tent of the Testimony, was set up, the cloud covered it. From evening till morning the cloud above the tabernacle looked like fire. That is how it continued to be; the cloud covered it, and at night it looked like fire. Whenever the cloud lifted from above the Tent, the Israelites set out; wherever the cloud settled, the Israelites encamped. At the Lord's command the Israelites set out, and at his command they encamped . . .
>
> 'Whether the cloud stayed over the tabernacle for two days or a month or a year, the Israelites would remain in camp and not set out; but when it lifted, they would set out.' (Numbers 9:15–18, 22)

John cited the Israelites' obedience to the Lord's command as an example of how we too need to be ready to move at a moment's notice. The cloud is God's glory; for Christians, believers in God's New Covenant, the cloud of glory or pillar of fire is the Holy Spirit resting within us.

'You know the presence of God gives you a peace and assurance which nothing on this earth can match. It's wonderful to be able to go to bed at night and lie at peace knowing you're where God wants you to be.'

Thus while we know this peace and assurance in a certain place, we should stay there. A former student, who had been called to Roffey and enjoyed her time there, used to feel that the buildings and landscape were suffused with glory. When she knew she was called to move on, they suddenly appeared ordinary: 'It's just bricks and trees now,' she said. For her, this was the outward sign that God's glory had moved on to the next stage of her life.

If we go where God is, it becomes the place of His rest. Jesus' disciples were told quite clearly where they should be to carry out His commands. There was a time when Jesus told them to stay in Jerusalem, a time when He told them to go to the Gentiles, and a time to go to the Jews.

Following the pillar of fire is a daily act of obedience, just as the Israelites did not know if they were pitching camp for one night or one year. John pointed out that one could be called away from Roffey for a day – or permanently.

'Sometimes you wonder why you are in one place for what seems so long, but calls vary. Abraham was called to stay and become a father, Paul had a call to go. Indeed, Paul could rarely stay to enjoy the fruits of his labours – every time he established a church, he had to move on. Sometimes God got the Jews to throw stones at him to make him go!' said John.

Margaret Powell, who spent two terms at Roffey, believes that the time apart is valuable not only for spiritual development but for forging new approaches and attitudes to working life. In her case, having to leave behind the trappings and routine of the business world was a redemptive process:

'Often a person becomes a Christian during their working life; others have the privilege of having an interruption in their career and being able to do a 'bulk dump' (a computer main-frame term which denotes wiping clean all active files)!

'Those who have not been through this redemptive process tend to carry on in grooves unless or until faced with the challenges that I faced. If I hadn't had the opportunity to make a break in my career, the same habits would have continued unchallenged, even though I was born again and filled with the Spirit. I have understood that walking with the Lord in working life is not just a question of observing the ten commandments, such as not fiddling expenses, using the phone and listening to gossip, but being what I would call 'radical', listening to the Lord and doing things His way when the world's work system screams just the opposite. This is where we really rule and reign as Christians and dominate the spiritual atmosphere. An example of this would be refusing a contract because, whilst the business proposed might appear to be 'ethical', you know God is telling you that in His eyes, it is not. In my case it meant putting a very lucrative assignment on the line because I insisted on a deadline which fitted in with my commitment to an intercession group, which I told them about! They looked slightly dazed, but admired my integrity and gave me the job anyway.

'It was a privilege to spend time apart with the Lord, letting him change all of my life priorities, melting down my identity, and just laying my career on the altar. I was prepared to never work in business again. So when, at the end of two terms, the Lord told me to return to the working world, I was able to obey in the confidence that the Lord had chosen to resurrect my "career". However, in my mind I don't have a career any more. What I do have is an exciting daily collaboration with the Lord which has led me to do more challenging work than ever before. In addition I find I am spiritually equipped to meet the challenges of a radically new approach to work.'

The call on leaders

The Christian is called to live in the power of God's word. To do that he must study the scriptures, and ask the Holy Spirit for enlightenment; revelation will also come from anointed teachers.

Leaders have considerable responsibility in this respect; they must lead their people while faithfully preaching God's word, whether or not it is what they want to hear. Since leaving Luton, Colin has had a ministry to church leaders in Britain and overseas, including holding weeks for leaders at The Hyde and Roffey Place where they are encouraged to hear God rather than hear about Him. Two conferences are now held each year for leaders who share Kingdom Faith's vision for revival. Although Colin would rather encourage and build up leaders than criticise them, he often warns them against reproducing themselves in their congregations. He emphasises the need for anointing to accompany a call: 'You shouldn't be doing anything without anointing. Who gives a person his ministry? God. Men often try to raise themselves up in ministry, but that's futile.'

Often he receives letters from people who in effect are saying, 'Can you raise me up in ministry? I've got this amazing call from God and I don't know how to put it into operation.'

Colin's answer is an emphatic 'no'; God will raise up the person with a call: 'It's not for me to play God in other people's lives.'

Colin's own ministry is an example of how God will raise up one man. When his Luton church was moving in revival, he went to his first charismatic conference. Looking at the speakers on the platform, something inside him said, 'You will be up front there.'

His response was disbelieving because he was still a basically shy, reserved person. In fact it is his shyness which has made him more obedient to God and hesitant about speaking anything which he does not feel has come from God. So he had no wish to be 'up front', because he would have felt 'totally, utterly inadequate'. Yet the next time there was a national conference, about two years later, he was one of the principal speakers.

'That was God, prophetically stirring, showing me what He was going to do with me.'

Since it is God who gives anointing, we must guard against jealousy. Colin warns against coveting another person's anointing for the wrong reasons. Sometimes, however, God can use someone as a role model for you.

'You see someone's anointing and the Spirit in you stirs in recognition that God is going to do something similar with you to get you longing for and seeking that anointing. But there's no way in which you could create your own anointing. Lots of people devise their own ministries, but there isn't that anointing, the stamp of God's divine enabling, on it.'

Submission to authority

Submission to authority is a necessity both for leaders and followers. As Colin bluntly puts it, 'You'll only have as much authority as you're submitted to authority. The devil counterfeits the real thing and reproduces authority as authoritarianism in many churches: hence leaders lord it over people. But submission to God's authority gives leaders real authority which everyone will recognise.'

> 'Obey your leaders and submit to their authority. They keep watch over you as men who must give an account. Obey them so that their work will be a joy, not a burden, for that would be of no advantage to you.' (Hebrews 13:17)

After more than two decades travelling around Britain and abroad to churches seeking renewal, Colin believes these lines have been abused in ungodly ways.

'Leaders lord it over congregations because they have been appointed to an ecclesiastical position. Elders usurp the authority of the individual Christian. This is not to say that anyone should refuse to submit to their leadership; no-one is meant to go round saying, "I don't have to submit to anyone because I'm submitted to Jesus so I only do what He tells me to."'

'If God wanted you to be a leader He'd make you one because He is all-powerful and can do so. Church meetings where everyone has a say are out of biblical order; the Church is *not* a democracy! It's to be led by people hearing from God. As one body, we function together and cannot all be the eyes. If we criticise our leaders, we're treading on the most dangerous ground possible because by so doing we are *judging God* for placing them over us.'

A constant, sobering awareness for Colin is the knowledge that one day he will have to give an account to God of how he has led the people brought to him. Yet this is a necessary awareness because it means the fear of God rather than the fear of man is paramount in his thinking.

'Leaders who don't have a fear of God but of man are

the authoritarian ones, the ones who encourage fear of man to make life easier for themselves,' he says.

Colin often asks God why his ministry has been so blessed when he says the same things as many others; the answer is that he can only speak with the authority that God gives him. 'Like earthly leaders, God wants to be able to trust people so He chooses the ones who will do what they're told, as they're told. That's why Jesus commended the centurion because he understood obedience and knew he had no authority to change His orders.

'When you're submitted to God you become a catalyst for God's enabling. So when you're praying for someone to be healed you can only say the words that *God* has given you with conviction and authority. So you bring a word with that authority and see a miracle – it's God's doing. The authority in your leadership depends *totally* on your personal walk with God.'

Wholehearted surrender

Sometimes, not least for those in leadership, it can become apparent that there is an area of their lives which they have not wholeheartedly surrendered to Christ. An example of this came up for Colin personally in early June 1992.

While he knew he had been living a life of obedience to the Holy Spirit for many years, Colin became aware that in the last few years he had not lived in the full blessing he had known from God in the last revival. Thus he sought God in anguish of spirit. The Lord reminded him of his call, to preach to the nations, which he received in 1970 with the warning 'If you do not speak, no-one will hear.'

At the time, it was almost the last thing Colin wanted to hear. When God showed him the implications of what that call would mean, it sounded like nothing that Colin desired or could make happen himself:

'No fibre of my being wanted what God was saying. I was content to remain a parish priest.'

Reminded now, twenty-two years later, of his call in

1970, Colin received a revelation from the Lord about Jesus' prayers in the Garden of Gethsemane. Colin had wondered why Jesus had to go to His Father three times and pray the same words each time: 'Abba, Father, everything is possible for you. Take this cup from me. Yet not what I will, but what you will.' (Mark 14:36)

The Lord showed Colin that Jesus knew His Father's will about the cross, yet like us He had free will. Faced with the reality of this, the culmination of God's purpose for His earthly life, it was necessary to wholeheartedly assent to this part of His call.

'It wasn't good enough to grudgingly accept the cross,' explained Colin. 'He had to break through to a new place in prayer of wanting it to happen.'

Like Jesus in Gethsemane, Colin also had to 'pray through' to the point where he joyfully accepted his Father's will for him.

> 'Therefore, since we are surrounded by such a great cloud of witnesses, let us throw off everything that hinders and the sin that so easily entangles, and let us run with perseverance the race marked out for us. Let us fix our eyes on Jesus, the author and perfecter of our faith, who for the *joy* set before him endured the cross, scorning its shame, and sat down at the right hand of the throne of God. Consider him who endured such opposition from sinful men, so that you will not grow weary and lose heart.' (Hebrews 12:2–3) (italics mine)

In the Garden of Gethsemane, Jesus knew what His Father's will for Him was – He had known since before Creation, when God the Father, the Son and the Holy Spirit had jointly planned the crucifixion. It was Jesus, the living Word of God, who inspired Isaiah to write the famous verses about the Messiah. (Isaiah 53)

A personal Gethsemane

Yet Jesus, the man, had to do more than accede to God's will; He had to face it with joy.

'The agony of Gethsemane meant that crucifixion, becoming sin and enduring separation from the Father with whom He had enjoyed the closest communion from an early age (eg the young Jesus' wise replies to learned men in the temple), was easy by comparison,' explained Colin. 'Scripture promises us that we will not have to sweat blood like Jesus did in the Garden, but for all of us there is a Gethsemane to face. Some may be resigned to God's will, some may not have prayed into being what He wants. The reason we all struggle with our heart attitudes is that we haven't faced our Gethsemane. It's possible to be a Spirit-filled, born-again believer and know that inevitably you will be raised in glory and see Jesus as He is according to His promise (Revelation 22:4) – and yet walk in disobedience, compromise and unrighteousness.

'In other words, you know the ultimate outcome of your life but you're not enjoying the path that leads to it!'

In 1 Peter 1:2 we read that Christians, God's elect, have been chosen 'according to the foreknowledge of God the Father, through the sanctifying work of the Spirit, for obedience to Jesus Christ and sprinkling by his blood'.

Colin believes this denotes not only cleansing but consecration.

'There's both a man-ward and God-ward aspect to consecration. Jesus had to make the act of offering and yielding – not a once-for-all act, in fact; He did it several times during His ministry.

'God wanted Jesus to face up to the implications of obedience and submit *joyfully*. God's purpose for you is to walk in holiness and righteousness *now*,' says Colin.

Jesus had to prove it is possible for a man living in righteousness ('godly fear' is the NKJV translation) to be obedient and therefore to be our representative and be made perfect. Submission to crucifixion was the highest act of faith (and obedience), springing from the knowledge that God would raise Him.

The Kingdom Faith team was encouraged to work through their individual 'Gethsemanes', resolving any issues which inhibited their freedom in the Lord.

'Working through your Gethsemane,' says Colin, 'is the ultimate expression of submission to God's authority.

This was the secret of how Jesus exercised His authority. The temptations in the wilderness were an attempt by Satan to get Him to act independently of His Father. Just one act of self-will (like Adam in Eden) would have made Him as big a sinner as the rest of us.'

The joy of full submission

An example of someone who had been through their Gethsemane and broken through to new joy and peace, the products of faith, was eighty-four-year-old Ted whom Colin met at a healing conference.

Ted became a Christian in his sixties; he and his wife changed their lifestyle drastically to become people of prayer. Yet this was not enough for them. Two years earlier, aged eighty-two, Ted had realised that his life was not totally given to the Lord. So he made what was far more than a fresh 'commitment' by praying, 'Lord, I only want your will for my life. I will submit myself to you. I surrender my self-will to you – I'll no longer exercise it for myself.'

Colin stressed that Ted's prayer is not the passive 'Thy will be done' which is born of unbelief. It is an active desire to lay down all that characterises the *self*.

Since then Ted's life has been transformed. 'I was refused permission to fight in the war because of poor health but since I asked God to take control of my life I've never been healthier.'

These days Ted believes it is his calling to attend conferences and encourage people. Often he drives up to three hundred miles alone. 'I never have to have a care or a thought for myself and never have to pray for myself because I'm so well taken care of now I'm in God's will.'

Amongst various messages the Lord gave to Ted and his wife was the revelation that He desired complete control of their lives, which could only be achieved by their giving up their own will. Ted realised that free will is given to us so that we can surrender it to Jesus. 'It's an unconditional surrender of body, mind and spirit.'

Ted now knows that nothing can happen to him which God has not allowed. 'You don't have any problems when you live like this because you know God is in complete control. I know that circumstances which appear adverse now will work out to my good. There's no other way to live the Christian life.'

Ted admits that many Christians do not understand his talking in this fashion. Perhaps they are where he used to be two years earlier, believing they are committed to God but convinced that He is not too concerned with every area of their lives. Perhaps they have even prayed Ted's prayer in response to a minister's invitation, and certainly at Roffey the words 'God desires to have control over every area of your lives' have been spoken frequently at meetings, both by platform speakers and as prophecy from the listeners.

So why are so many Christians unable to talk about God like this? Simply, Colin maintains, because God knows the attitudes of our hearts; He knows if we mean what we pray! When He knows that we truly want what He wants, He comes and gives us the grace to do it; He will accomplish it for us.

God's call on women

People who often feel they need a double dose of grace are mothers. Women who believe they may have certain spiritual gifts that would benefit their church can feel frustrated by the demands of their home and family. In a church which is clearly moving forward with God, the conflict can be especially trying.

For Caroline Urquhart there was never a debate. She was a wife and mother before she became a Christian, and soon after that realised that her call was to support Colin and be available for her family and others God had called into their household.

Family comes first, though. Caroline admits that she and Colin have sometimes been so busy attending to others' spiritual and material needs that they have neglected their own children, 'but God brought us back'. Not having time for their own family was painful.

'God doesn't give you family for you to ignore them. Some young mums think that the only ministry they can have is going out to pray with or counsel people, while their poor family is at home desperately needing them.'

Ensuring the house is clean and the washing done is all part of her personal call to support Colin in the call God has given him.

'If I do things which cause me to neglect what I should be doing as a wife, that's not right. Ideally everything at home should be in order before you go out.'

Neglect can cause clergy children to go off the rails. Caroline has seen other ministers' wives with young children in conflict over pursuing their own external ministry.

Although she believes that people have to weigh up their own priorities and callings, she sees being married and having children as a privilege for women.

'I personally feel that if you're in that privileged position, you should care for your husband and children and home. When all that is accomplished, you can go and do this, that and the other for God. When my children were small I used to think they'd never grow up and I'd never be able to do anything for God, but once they start going to school you can do other things that God wants.'

Putting the home first, not as a drudgery but a privilege, is the recipe for a happy Christian family, according to Caroline.

'As long as you're providing a good, open home with a warm atmosphere and your children know they're loved and cared for, you're fulfilling God's will. You need the company of other mums, too.'

She uses the example of the woman in Proverbs 31 who is so capable that her husband is always talking about her:

'God's not asking women to deny their gifts and talents but to use them wisely, as He leads. Any man who wants to subjugate his wife into a skivvie is totally wrong. Each woman will blossom in doing different things; it's just a question of finding the areas in which you are anointed.

'But at the end of the day you've been entrusted with bringing up children in the fear of the Lord – and what calling is higher?'

Caroline and others at Kingdom Faith feel that there is

often unnecessary tension between those who are called to full-time ministry and those doing secular jobs. Many who start work at Kingdom Faith have assumed there would be plenty of time for preaching and healing the sick; in fact they are more likely to be dealing with the practical side of keeping a ministry afloat such as packing up cassette tapes, washing cars or answering the phone.

Dan Chesney pointed out that those in secular employment had many more opportunities to share their faith. God did not want everyone to down tools because a revival was on the way. 'God is going to work through you in your everyday life. Your job is your ministry. A small percentage of Christians are called into "Christian" work; meanwhile God is looking for the everyday hero: the computer programmer, the housewife, the lorry driver, the secretary.'

As Ray McCauley told an audience of Christians drawn from all over Britain to the Kingdom Faith Camp, 'You weren't born to *find* an assignment, but *because* of an assignment. God saw revival coming to England and decided to create you for the revival.'

Too often we wait for words and visions before realising that we are probably where God wants us to be. We simply have to realise that God is already using us as we do our daily work.

In the meantime, we can ensure we are in the right place with God so He can use us more fully.

'If you don't know your call yet, submit reverently to God and you soon will,' is how Colin sums up guidance for Christians. 'The death of your self-will can be long drawn-out and painful – or quick.'

Chapter Three

LOVE ONE ANOTHER

He answered, "'Love the Lord your God with all your heart and with all your soul and with all your strength and with all your mind'; and, 'Love your neighbour as yourself.'" (Luke 10:27)

Nations are changed when people's hearts are changed. Jesus did not preach about the social issues of His day, but aimed His words at people's hearts, knowing that hearts of love and compassion would alter everything they did.

'The love we have for one another will change the nation – and we can only do it through God,' is an accepted maxim at Kingdom Faith. It was 'Faith working through love' (Galatians 5:6) which became the motto of Kingdom Faith Ministries. Love prevents faith becoming selfish, because the believer's faith will be directed outwards rather than focussing exclusively on personal needs and wants. In turn love is ineffectual without faith because 'everything that does not come from faith is sin'. (Romans 14:23)

God is love; revival is God's people living in the fullness of the truth. Therefore revival will see an abundance of love.

During the revival at The Hyde in 1981, all those present were made deeply aware of the power of God's love touching their hearts. And that love was to spill out to their relationships with others.

For Pam Hunt, the depth of love at that time mirrored what she had read in the book of Acts.

'It was laying down your lives for one another, loving and caring for them and sharing your possessions. People were different after that.'

Nonetheless, such love can only flow freely outwards when it is rooted in a strong relationship with God. After all, if every Christian in a body of believers really was walking and talking with Jesus all day, they would be enjoying permanent corporate revival!

In order to change, some people need a revelation of God's love; in the meantime they doubt that God wants to hear from them.

Colin responds to this by reminding students of their need to build up their relationship with God.

'God doesn't want to hear from us only when we need something, like cats – we're His children and He longs to hear from us! If you're in love with God, you won't want to miss your daily time with Father. And if the devil reminds you it's your day off, tell him that God loves you on Saturdays too!'

He also issues a warning:

'Every time you criticise or judge someone or go back to sleep in the morning instead of spending time with the Lord, you're demonstrating your lack of relationship with God.'

Jesus' closeness to His heavenly Father was proved by His obedience to death, 'even death on a cross.' (Philippians 2:8) If Jesus was busy with ministry all day, He went away to pray all night. 'He didn't dare do a thing without the Father. If He had done one little thing independent of God, it would have been sin and we wouldn't be saved here today.'

For Christian leaders (and all Kingdom Faith students are leaders-in-waiting), this is their most powerful role model: 'Jesus never expected of others what He was not living and never preached what He didn't practise.'

Colin also teaches his students that it is utterly pointless to try to copy someone else's ministry, because the secret of other people's success lies in their concern to do exactly what God tells them. When speaking at international conferences Colin has met many Christian leaders who were completely humble and self-effacing, quite different from the person they appeared to be on the conference platform. 'They're so concerned for what God's saying, and meeting the needs of people, that they can appear to be brash. In fact they're fallible people to whom tough things happen; they get more persecution and endure greater trials of faith.' So the state of your heart is a key to how much God can use you.

Intimate love

The intimacy of God's love was a revelation for David Hazeldine, a robust eighteen-year-old whose two terms at Roffey and Lamplugh House greatly increased the depth of his relationship with God. Now he uses all the Bible's poetry and Jesus' descriptive words to express his love for God in his quiet times. His favourite book of the Bible is the Song of Songs, to which he was drawn in an unexpected way during a time of public worship at Spring Harvest. The Holy Spirit said to him, 'Stop worshipping; I want to tell you something.' When David had stopped and was standing still amongst four thousand singing Christians, the Holy Spirit told him, 'Jesus is the fairest of ten thousand.'

Although it took David two days to find the reference (Song of Songs 5:10, AV), its meaning sank into him immediately. He knew if Jesus walked into that room He would be the most beautiful person there, the one he would most want to look at and worship. 'I just found myself saying His name, 'Jesus', over and over again in tears for forty-five minutes.'

On the last day of his term at Roffey, the Lord said to David, 'I am your lover.'

David was slightly taken aback. 'I'm an eighteen-year-old boy and you're a male God. That's a bit funny, Lord! People might think I'm crazy if I say you're my lover.'

Yet in the next two to three months David's relationship with God deepened to the extent that he described it as a love affair. One of the things Jesus said to His Father is particularly enlightening: 'I have made you known to them, and will continue to make you known in order that the love you have for me may be in them and that I myself may be in them.' (John 17:26)

David realised that as one of 'them', a disciple of Jesus, the Father's love for Jesus was in him too.

'Over the holidays and during the following term at Lamplugh House, Jesus was revealing to me how much the Father loved Him and then the Holy Spirit was whispering, "Look, this is what you desire. This is what you need." So I've been in a love affair with Jesus. The Song of Songs has been my favourite book and I just continue to read it. I know it's poetry which to most blokes of eighteen is a soft thing, but if you've got the love of God inside you, you want to be with Him.

'I find myself talking to Jesus as if I'm talking to my fiancée. Sometimes I finish writing a letter to her and end up praying it to the Lord!'

One test of obedience came when the Holy Spirit first asked him to bow down during worship. 'That was the hardest thing for me to do because I thought everyone would be staring at me. So I said, "OK, Lord, I'll do it for you – not for these other people."'

David believes that God has made him a promise about the impending revival; it will be totally centred around the person of Jesus. 'People will be in awe of Jesus. The pull of Jesus will be so strong that you won't want to do anything but what He wants. You'll desire to love others just to please the Lord, and you'll desire to give prophecies in a meeting where you've previously been too scared.'

Fearless love

> 'There is no fear in love. But perfect love drives out fear, because fear has to do with punishment. The one who fears is not made perfect in love.' (1 John 4:18)

God's love will cast out fear, but we have to know it in our spirits first. Some fear that God cannot love them; a history of rejection and abuse has convinced them they are unlovable. How are they to cross the divide which separates them from receiving Jesus' love?

'There's only one way to know whether God loves you or not – you believe it!' says Colin. 'You can go for endless ministry and counselling, all of which concentrates your mind on yourself, which the devil loves. The last thing Satan wants is for you to feel secure, so he encourages you to dwell on your past record and current failings, then to compare yourself with others. Get your eyes on Jesus; repent of doubting His love and believe the truth that He gave His life for *you*.'

Is it really as simple as that? Yes, but it takes some longer than others to receive it! Colin emphasises that believers need to immerse themselves in the truth to see the renewing of their minds. 'The more you believe it, the more you'll live in the good of it.'

He also recommends speaking the words from John 15:9 for five minutes a day, using the prayer method described in *Listen & Live*.[1]

'As the Father has loved me, so have I loved you. Now remain in my love.'

In fact criticism has been directed at Colin for the simplicity of this aspect of his teaching. But he points out that Jesus' message was simple: 'Repent and believe.' Combing the gospels for his *Direct Counselling* course, he was repeatedly struck by the directness of Jesus' teaching. There was no going back over the 'victim's' past, just the truth administered with compassion. And people were set free by the truth, because that is one of Jesus' promises.

During prayer one day, the Holy Spirit asked Colin a question:

'Did Jesus counsel His disciples?'

Of course the answer was that Jesus *taught* them the Kingdom principles which would make them secure in God's love. Today His disciples have His word and the inner witness of the Holy Spirit providing and confirming the truth. Over the years Colin and Caroline have seen many people's lives gloriously transformed because, even if they came from 'the gutters of life', they believed the revelation that nothing could separate them from the love of God, and they understood that believing in that love was an active process; it was theirs for the taking.

Lack of security in God's love means we are tempted to compare ourselves with others. It is especially important that a community of believers, whether a college or church, should be united. Colin relies on a simple standard: he tries not to say anything behind a person's back that he could not say to their face. His teaching on criticism is too true for comfort:

'If you don't know the security of God's love, you feel jealous of those who are secure and are motoring with Him. You get very critical of them and home in on anything you can find to criticise about them.'

This insecurity is accompanied by an innate desire to prove oneself right, i.e. self-righteousness, because discovering one was wrong increases the sense of failure which gave rise to the critical attitude!

Once we open up our hearts to receive more of God's love we can give it out to others, which is God's original intention. And when Colin has been harshly criticised, he has found that God has provided other people to love and encourage him.

Forgiving love

When talking about forgiveness, Colin has memorably likened the Christian's mind to a computer. All of us have a collection of 'negative' files from past failures and hurts. But when we are born again, God opens a new file with one entry: 'Jesus'. The Jesus file is an enormous file, full of love, patience, power and miracles. We can plug into this programme day by day – why plug into any other?

The only trouble is, there's also a blank key put there by Satan which we can't resist pressing. And each time we press it, our minds whizz out of the Jesus file and back into 'self' – self-accusation, self-condemnation, hurts, resentment, failure, fears, sickness and symptoms.

'If you're fool enough you'll believe it,' says Colin. 'If we keep no files or records of negative things, Satan can't write on our screens. Make the decision to close existing negative files so when he comes to remind you of them, tell him the file's erased for good, you've forgiven and you are forgiven, and now you're operating in the Jesus file!'

The devil will lie to us, often successfully, by making us think that a certain hurt is too deep to forget. But Jesus says, 'You can abide in me *now*, by choosing to keep no record of wrongs now; you're loved, forgiven, accepted and made holy; why are you fooling around in that other programme?'

What most of us take time to grasp is that we can return to the Jesus programme at the flick of a mental button.

On that particular occasion Colin invited his listeners to deliberately 'close' certain files, which for many was a liberating experience: 'It is for freedom that Christ has set us free.' (Galatians 5:1)

Likening our mind to a computer in this way is a clear illustration of the difference between soul and spirit. Both Colin and Dan have taught extensively on this difference to highlight the fact that we have an hourly and daily choice whether to 'walk in the Spirit' or in the flesh. The flesh is our 'old self'; walking in the Spirit is to assume our new identity made possible by Jesus' shed blood. Paul tells the Colossians that they have taken off their old self and put on the new self, which is being renewed in knowledge in the image of its Creator. (Colossians 3:9–10) Dan explained how Jesus walked solely in the Spirit – which made Him a radical.

Jesus' sacrifice was the perfect example of selflessness; there was no self-motivation in the cross. 'When you're operating in the soul, there's always an element of self in it which wants to dominate others so they cringe or are in your debt', explains Colin.

Soul and spirit

Walking in the Spirit is not something that comes automatically to most Christians, which is one of the reasons we do not see revival. As Dan pointed out, 'As long as you're a carnal Christian, you're still in crèche.'

This teaching came during the October 1992 revival week, just before the Kingdom Faith community began to see the first signs of spiritual breakthrough. Deciding to put the self to death (Colossians 3:5), and to deny themselves daily signalled the start of a personal breakthrough for many, no matter how much they had previously thought their soul was under control.

'The soul is used to being in charge and won't give up easily; hence Paul's struggle in Romans 7,' Dan taught. 'Train yourself to be spiritual all the time, not just at certain times. Have you noticed how some people take spiritual holidays at certain times of the day? You might be clapping and lifting your arms in church, happily operating in the Spirit, but when you leave church, woe betide anyone who tries to leave the car park before you!'

As the father of three, he knows that for many women the difficult time to walk in the Spirit is between 5 and 7 p.m. when they have to get children to bed and make dinner!

The soul loves to be built up by praise, whereas for Jesus the only praise He would accept came from His Father.

'One way or another,' said Colin, 'God will get you to the same place where you won't even listen to flattery. While you matter to yourself, you'll be full of self-concern. The secret of God using you is to know you're nothing apart from your identity in Christ, which is yours only by His grace.'

While coping with criticism, Colin has also had to learn to cope with praise from men and women, which is possibly harder to handle. For years he has had an 'inbuilt system' that does not allow him to accept men's praise for himself; when congratulated on a fine address, he tries to say something that deflects the glory to God. 'If you don't give the glory to God, the enemy will get in and try to make you think you're something.'

A previous recipient of teaching on the soul and spirit was Marigold Pym at The Hyde:

'Colin started teaching from Watchman Nee's book, *The Spiritual Man*. Up to that time, I'd always thought they were the same thing – I'd had no idea about the soul life being completely different to the spiritual life, and it was just like a bombshell to me. I could see that I'd hardly been a Christian at all before that! I was filled with the Spirit, but practically everything I did seemed to be at the soul level.'

Marigold is able to laugh now at the memory of her first three months at The Hyde as she faced up to this new challenge of obeying the promptings of the Holy Spirit rather than the inclinations of her soul (consisting of the intellect, will and emotions). The motives she now saw as soulish were suddenly exposed as she lived through the consequences of Hebrews 4:12: 'For the word of God is living and active. Sharper than any double-edged sword, it penetrates even to dividing soul and spirit, joints and marrow; it judges the thoughts and attitudes of the heart.'

'Quite honestly,' said Marigold, 'I was devastated and I spent our first three months in the community just crying! Colin was very good and explained things. At that time he often used to arrange to see us individually to talk about where we were; I always seemed to be going to his study and getting sorted out! So this was a major advance which changed me completely.'

God's love is a spiritual love; and it is only the Holy Spirit in us who will help us love when our emotions cannot stretch to encompass all that we are called to love.

'God's love isn't gooey and sentimental,' says Colin, 'but strong and real. The cry of my heart is to see more and more of His love manifest in my life, so His love fills all my prayers. God made it clear to me there's no limit to His love and the only one who limits that love is me.'

He highlights the difference between two sorts of love described in the New Testament Greek: the verb *phileo*, which means 'I love with tender affection', and *agape*, used to describe God's love – faithful, steadfast love which never fails because it is born of the Spirit. In the famous passage where Jesus asks Peter if he loves Him, Jesus is requesting *agape* love, while Peter can only respond with '*phileo*'.

The love which we are to give back to God is *agape,* and it was a shock to many of Colin's hearers to realise that while they could say they loved Jesus, it was with tender affection; not the *agape* which is rightly His. Once we love God with that *agape* love, we can start to love anybody and everything, regardless of how unlovable they are. *Agape* does not count the cost of loving, whereas loving according to the strength of our feelings *(phileo)* is, by definition, limited by the flesh.

The expression of religious love, according to Colin, is *phileo*; it is rooted in sentiment rather than spirit, so 'it likes nice quiet music and pleasant feelings'.

Getting real with God is not helped by performance prayers. 'Mary', who worked at Roffey for two years, found herself speaking for the whole body in her prayers; even in her own quiet times with God she found herself saying, 'We praise you, Lord'. It came as a shock when Colin announced one morning that from now on everyone should pray 'I' prayers, addressing God in the first person. 'You can't express anyone else's heart desire and "Amen" at the end doesn't necessarily mean others are agreeing with you', he told them. Mary realised she had been hiding behind her 'we' prayers.

'You have to say what's on your heart. If that's frustration, that's what you say to the Lord.'

Praying the Scriptures also helped her establish a better love relationship with God. In at least 50 per cent of prayer meetings held before main meetings at Roffey, participants pray through passages of Scripture. Personalising certain verses emphasised her uniqueness in God's eyes:

'*I* have been chosen according to the foreknowledge of God the Father, through the sanctifying work of the Spirit, for obedience to Jesus Christ and sprinkling by his blood.' (1 Peter 1:2)

'Before I formed you in the womb I knew you, before you were born I set you apart.' (Jeremiah 1:5)

As Mary was an orphan, the deep truth of such scriptures provided reassurance which no amount of well-meaning human consolation could have done. She found the blessings and curses section of Deuteronomy 28 provided excellent prayers for herself and the church; praying that the fruit of her womb would be blessed and her kneading baskets full (financial provision) was also an excellent way of absorbing God's promises for those who obey Him.

Loving as an act of your will is *agape* love, which does not hold back until it feels like loving.

When Dan and Nori Chesney first came to Britain, they had plenty of opportunity to put *agape* love into practice. They discovered the British did not care for Dan's style, from his ministry tapes to his ties (both were rather loud). It seemed as if they were being criticised for everything.

But instead of retreating they determined, every morning, that 'in the name of Jesus we shall love the British today'. It took six months to see a change in people's attitudes, but it worked in the end.

Love in practice

It is *agape* love that has to flow out to others, not only to those close to us but to the rest of the world. The Kingdom Faith leadership, along with many other leaders, know that the world will be affected by the sight of a body of people who are committed to love each other, no matter how different they may be in calling, age, tastes, education, intellectual abilities and social background. They agree that this depth of love will have even more impact on outsiders than the healings and miracles which will abound in revival.

Once a body of people is unified, the strength of their *agape* love for each other will want to find expression in caring for the outside world. Colin knows that revival brings an extra compassion for the poor and needy which cannot be manufactured; for this reason he teaches the importance of adapting and submitting to each other within the body of Christ; while we are still counting the cost of submission to God and others, we may find ourselves acting independently of God by choosing and doing good works our way, instead of God's way. It is well-meant, but there is still a large element of 'self' in our motives, which is ultimately unsatisfactory for ourselves and for God. 'Faith without works is dead', but Colin teaches that it is important to ensure you are helping others for God's sake, rather than as a means of salving your conscience, or even out of a desire to prove yourself to God and to others!

'Revival begins, not in the world, but in God's own people. Their hearts are revived, brought back to life with the holiness and love of Jesus. A necessary condition for such revival is repentance for all that is unholy in the believer's life. Some of these things he may be aware of; others will be hidden from him because the heart is so deceitful. There will be deep motives of pride and selfishness which he may not recognise, but which lie behind all he does in the name of God.'[2]

Hence it is important to let *God* lead us into 'the good works which He has planned in advance for us to do'. (Ephesians 2:10)

Social care is one of God's instructions to Kingdom Faith Church, which He made very clear to Colin through the words of Isaiah:

> 'Is not this the kind of fasting I have chosen:
> to loose the chains of injustice
> and untie the cords of the yoke,
> to set the oppressed free
> and break every yoke?
> Is it not to share your food with the hungry
> and to provide the poor wanderer with shelter –
> when you see the naked, to clothe him,
> and not to turn away from your own flesh and blood?
> Then your light will break forth like the dawn,
> and your healing will quickly appear.'
> (Isaiah 58: 6–8)

While the church is growing, it is hard to give numbers of those involved in helping the needy, but there is a particular concern for drug addicts, a problem in parts of the local area. A group of men felt led to open a café and drop-in centre in a particularly deprived area where the lack of facilities meant young people were especially prey to drug dealers. The church is helped by growing out of an existing ministry which already had people active in leading school assemblies and visiting prisons. Each week of term-time there are at least two local school assemblies taken by Kingdom Faith people; this ministry is led by Harry Creswell, who combines it with his roles as Church Administrator and Faith Camp organiser. The prison ministry began with Elizabeth Allan and Joy Pedder, providing a perfect combination of Kingdom Faith team and church members working together. They hold services in prisons with the help of musicians, singers and actors both from the team and the church, who feel called to prison work.

God's love in marriage

While none of us can earn our salvation, we can all let God's love effect the changes He desires to see in our lives. Too often we want to change others rather than ourselves, but changing others is impossible unless by love and encouragement, a lesson particularly helpful for wives of non-Christian husbands.

When Pam Hunt became part of the fellowship at The Hyde, she almost despaired of her husband Tim ever becoming a Christian, although he would attend some meetings. After attempting to persuade him, she decided to spend more time praying about it. The change was not lost on Tim; he found it more and more difficult as things changed at home:

'It was the silence and the peace that finished me off in the end! Pam had actually stopped hounding me. So there was nothing to attack. I'd see the sublime, quiet smiles, and think, "Here we go again!"'

Soon afterwards he gave his life to Jesus and ultimately gave up his job to work at Roffey Place.

Unsaved husbands can become jealous of God, but the fact that God is jealous for His creation (Exodus 34:14) is often overlooked. He made Colin aware of His jealousy – which, once rid of its negative overtones can best be understood in terms of zealousness – during one of their night-time prayer sessions. (Colin's time is God's time, so when Colin is woken in the night, he goes off to pray.)

'I want you totally for myself,' God told Colin. 'Not even a part of you belongs to you or any other person – not your wife nor your children. I want you totally because I am a jealous God.'

Understandably, Colin's first reaction was, 'Hang on a minute, Lord.'

Then God started to explain it, having shocked him into giving his full attention.

'I paid the price for you. You have no right to hold on to any part of you *and nor has anybody else.*'

Whether Colin was married or not had nothing to do with it; God was stating a basic spiritual truth.

'I have the prerogative to do with you what I please. So I won't share you with anyone but I can decide to give you to someone or give someone to you. Yet I shall still be first.'

This is a truth Colin and Caroline have lived with for many years; after years in the ministry, they believe it is the key to a happy marriage. They have seen trouble often start in Christian marriages when husbands and wives seek the security from each other which can only be found in God. To create their security, they may want the home to revolve around them, at which point peace departs. Their demands usually involve manipulation, especially of those close to them. By seeking to replace Jesus as the home's central focus, they are unconsciously demanding to be worshipped, and rebelling against God's order.

Dan and Nori Chesney attribute the success of their sixteen-year-old marriage to putting Jesus first; every time Nori had a problem, Dan advised her to take it to God! Naturally they gave each other loving support, but neither expected the other to take care of their deepest hurts. Reliance on God rather than on another human strengthened both their marriage and their relationship, as they were able to give love freely rather than demand security from each other.

If any Christian has trouble acknowledging that their husband, wife or child belongs first and foremost to God, it is because they are not sure that *they* belong to Him themselves.

When Caroline Urquhart became a Christian ('Everybody in the parish was a Christian before I was!') she wrote a letter to Jesus, a task requested of new believers at that time (new Kingdom Faith students also write one). Doing this made her very aware that she had to release Colin to God. 'Colin belonged to God first and *then* he belonged to me.'

If she has ever tried to take Colin back again entirely for herself, their relationship has suffered and she gets hurt in the process. Shortly before their first grandchild was born, God confronted her afresh with the truth that they both belonged to Him. It was quite a battle to release him again, but she has been rewarded by a different relationship.

'If I'm expecting Colin to be to me or give to me all that I want him to be, then I am disappointed. And I'm forever going to be disappointed because he's an imperfect man! So my responsibility is to give to him, serve him and enable him in whatever way God wants and not to take from him. But that's also his responsibility towards me! So it has to be worked out on both sides.'

Caroline recognises that imbalance comes when one partner is giving more than the other. Her opinion is biblical and realistic.

'The husband is head of the household, and he is to love his wife as Christ loved the Church. If all men were like that, you'd have wonderful marriages – no wife would have any problem submitting to a man like that! Women should be in submission to their husbands, but the husband and wife must submit to one another; it means you willingly place yourself under someone else's authority.'

Caroline's wisdom about relationships has been gathered from many years of being married to a sought-after leader while living in an extended household. One of the key things she and Colin learned was the impossibility of they or anyone else trying to change their partner.

'You pray,' explains Caroline. 'If you view something about your husband or wife as negative, you ask God if you're right. If you are, you pray about it and you can actually see the Holy Spirit effect changes. Colin does the same for me; he'll pray rather than come and confront me. Occasionally we'll confront each other, but we're not always telling the other they've got to change! You can't build a relationship on that; it doesn't work.'

As a result of releasing each other, the tensions from a busy lifestyle are lessened. In one year Caroline's birthday and wedding anniversary were unexpectedly claimed by God for church prayer meetings. Everyone was blessed by her sacrifice as they met with God.

Christians often speculate on their life priorities, juggling God, family, church and work. Colin had always felt it a rather pointless discussion. God agreed:

'You're right. Your order (from top to bottom) should be God, God, God and God.'

Chapter Four

THE COST OF LOVE

'A new command I give you: Love one another. As I have loved you, so you must love one another. By this all men will know that you are my disciples, if you love one another.' (John 13:34–35)

'Unlike many teachers in the faith movement,' says intercessor Elizabeth Allan, 'Colin Urquhart preaches about the importance of having a servant heart. He doesn't just encourage everyone to get blessed and stop there.'

Caroline Urquhart agrees: 'Being a Christian isn't just getting born again and filled with the Spirit; it's righteousness, holiness, love and going out into all the world. And while you can have a church which is meeting and miracle-orientated, it's the life in the body of Christ which should change the nation.'

Commitment and unity are key concepts for the life of any church, and they are certainly essential prerequisites for revival, not only to influence the world with the purity and compassion of believers' lives, but to enable them to withstand opposition.

From the early 1970s, the Urquhart family have lived in a community of one sort or another. First they opened up their home to a family in need, then they lived in a sprawling community of families at The Hyde, followed by over six years in their own extended households nearby, and ended up at Roffey Place. It happened more by God's design than theirs, but it has ensured that Colin could preach what he was practising.

The lives of Colin's Luton parishioners were completely

changed when God gave him a set of principles by which they were to live.

> 'You are to commit your lives to Me – to be led by My Holy Spirit.
> 'You are to promise obedience to the leading of My Spirit within the Community.
> 'You are to worship and pray together in the Spirit.
> 'You are to love one another – have that relationship with one another that is pleasing to Me.
> 'You are to be concerned with the spreading of My Word of Truth in this parish.
> 'You are to show the quality of love I require of My children to Christians of other churches.
> 'I, the Lord, promise to lead you in all things – to enrich greatly your lives with many blessings, if you will only be faithful to Me in this. I will enter into an agreement with you, an agreement which I will honour because of My love for you. Let no one be afraid of entering into an agreement with Me, for by doing this you will be bound closer to Me in love.'[1]

By the time Colin was called away from St Hugh's in Luton, his congregation were leading 'very committed, sacrificial lives'. Over fifty families were sharing their wage packets, reflecting a depth of commitment which would have been impossible without the Holy Spirit's help!

This was not a lifestyle for the sake of being different; it came about in obedience to God's command. In turn the church saw miracles and healings which attracted people from all over the world to an otherwise unprepossessing town.

So for the Urquhart family the main difficulty in leaving St Hugh's was leaving behind that commitment of love.

'They were people who had learned to lay down their lives for one another, to live for one another and not themselves,' said Colin.

After being led by God into such a commitment, Colin was convinced that the test of your love for God was the extent to which you loved your neighbour.

'In the parable of the talents, the man with ten talents was successful and could be trusted. The ones who aren't trustworthy get nowhere, i.e. if you're burying your gifts and simply trying to survive. God gives success to those who live for others; if you're protective of yourself, you won't be successful. When you see what someone's getting back, not simply financially but in terms of kindness and love from others, you can see what they're giving.'

He knew that such a quality of living could only emerge from a group of people who had consciously committed themselves to one another:

'It can't be produced at a meeting; it can't be produced just by God anointing people. God fills people with the Holy Spirit *to enable that kind of lifestyle to develop* – but it's got to develop. When I left Luton I wanted to see that kind of love and commitment developing in churches all over the nation and wherever else God led me. The disappointment was to see how seldom that happened.'

Colin attributes this failure to lack of vision in the leadership of those churches that were being affected by the Holy Spirit.

'A congregation will only grow according to the leadership it's given. People were willing to be blessed and taught and to minister spiritual gifts, but it seemed that in nearly every situation there was a kind of stopping point; people were prepared to go thus far and no further.'

In fact Colin had led his Luton congregation through the same sticking-point, a tense time when some of the church were determined to resist further commitment to each other. Knowing the sort of commitment God was calling for, Colin resolutely went forward despite those who were afraid to follow. After a three-week period when none of the congregation could sing praises wholeheartedly because they were counting the potential personal cost of total commitment to each other, they acceded to God's request. 'Praise took off again after that,' Colin remembers.

As he travelled around the country in the early years after leaving Luton, he found he could hardly talk about churches making a commitment to one another because 'People weren't anywhere near ready for it.'

He had to do much more spadework than he had expected, teaching people how to move in the basic things of the Spirit, how to use the gifts and how to minister healing to one another. These were all the things St Hugh's had learned before reaching the point where they could unreservedly commit themselves to one another, though Colin stresses that such commitment would never have been possible without the Holy Spirit's help.

Invited more often than not to renew other men's churches, Colin became frustrated. 'Even in all the blessing that you saw happening there was this sense that this wasn't what it was all about.'

He was not ungrateful, however, for what God was doing at those early meetings:

'It was a great blessing to see a hundred or more people come to the Lord at a meeting, as was common, with hundreds of people baptised in the Holy Spirit and hundreds of people healed. You can only praise the Lord for changing all those lives.'

What Colin could not do as an itinerant speaker was to build those lives together. When he moved to The Hyde, it became very important to recreate the kind of lifestyle he had known at Luton. This would ensure that his ministry was emerging from the life and commitment being lived out there. The lifestyle was nothing less than New Testament Christianity, demonstrating the commitment to one another shown clearly in the Acts of the Apostles.

At its best, the love between believers is a powerful expression of the love of Christ. It was not unknown for non-Christians to be so affected by the atmosphere as they drove up to The Hyde that they sought the source of that love for themselves and would break down in meetings.

The Bethany Fellowship

The concept of 'community' is not one Colin has preached for its own sake, although the Bethany Fellowship at The Hyde came into being at a time when Christian communities became fashionable. Some were communities whose end was in themselves. However, the body of people at The Hyde were called there to support Colin's ministry, so they had a common purpose and task.

In doing their jobs, they were able to relate to each other and the world outside with a quality of love which became renowned in the Christian world; they even featured in a secular TV documentary. That quality of love was to be exported wherever Colin and team members travelled:

'The Lord showed me how important it was always to minister out of the life of the body, out of relationship. Anybody who's in itinerant ministry really needs to be ministering out of a body that is a reflection of what he is teaching. If he's not working out his teaching in relationship to others, then where is he? And even though air fares for overseas missions were costly, God would cover the cost.

'But I found a lot of people didn't understand this. Why should I have three or four people with me who weren't appearing on the platform, and who were not going to speak? But what counted was their presence, the fact we were united in faith and love as we prayed. We were a sort of microcosm of the life and commitment that the rest of us had to one another. That was how Jesus ministered, out of the microcosm of those twelve disciples. He fed the multitudes and of course ministered to a much greater number of disciples.

'If you look at what John says (John 13:12–13, 1 John 4:11–12), merely having a passing relationship with your brethren doesn't say much about your relationship with God.'

And it is by a committed body of people that the twentieth-century multitudes, some starving both spiritually and materially, will be helped.

'In revival, people's hearts are touched; they reach out almost instinctively to the poor and needy,' Colin has discovered.

The reputation of The Hyde drew many people to seek spiritual help there, which had been unobtainable elsewhere. This meant that the ministry team's attention was divided. Colin and Caroline, who had had people living in their house for several years, were used to the idea that there were some people who needed to be brought out of their own situations.

'You can't just pray over them and send them home,' Colin believes.

'People need to belong,' says Caroline. 'Those words were impressed on us when we first opened up our home. Some people may still feel they don't belong because they're not being handled or loved properly, but none of us is perfect.'

What happened next provides helpful guidelines for home-sharing. It was not rotas but heart attitudes which determined the level of harmony in a shared home.

At the time they never debated whether this was what God required of them, although the whole experience was a baptism of fire for Caroline. The discovery that she could not love people in her own strength caused her to call upon God for help and she was baptised in the Holy Spirit. (Her story is very honestly told in her book *His God, My God*.[2])

Now she had found a greater source of love than herself, but it still took time to get used to queuing for her bathroom and finding all the available seats in the sitting-room occupied.

In fact God had told her to release everything she could have called her own – husband, children, house, possessions – to Him shortly before He asked them to take the next step of laying down their lives in this very practical way.

This went beyond practising hospitality; it was a 'crash course in considering others before myself and learning how selfish I was'.

She discovered she had wanted things her way, and if she had not released her home to God it could have been much harder to accept the minor but meaningful differences in other people's outlooks; she had to realise that people were not implying contempt for her hospitality when they carried on using metal spoons on her carefully preserved saucepans and cluttering her previously clear kitchen window-sill.

'I wouldn't have said I found other people particularly difficult, but you're really challenged when you have to share everything you have. It's different if someone's coming to stay for a fortnight; you go out of your way to bless them by giving to them – because you know they're going to leave! Not knowing if or when they're going to leave puts a different complexion on the whole thing.'

At that time she did not know much about praying with others until God gave her a scripture one night which told her clearly she had not received help because she had not asked Him.

'I realised God was telling me to stop grumbling and start praying so He could sort out my problems.'

Gradually she saw solutions. To some extent, the challenge of sharing her home affected her more directly than Colin; he had the church and was often out, whereas her world was caring for her children in her home. Her availability, allied to her friendly, approachable nature meant that she had to spend hours listening to others' problems.

'One guy was rather depressive and I reproached myself for not being able to "minister" to him because I didn't understand his problems. God cut in and told me, "I didn't ask you to minister to him, simply to love him."'

All the pressure left her as she concentrated on loving him. Next time he started to talk to her, she found she could understand his problems. This was another proof that she had to do things God's way.

Working out one's commitment to God within a community is as significant in the comparatively new Kingdom Faith Church as it was in the days of the Bethany Fellowship. The principles for community living given by God to Colin in 1979 are as valid as ever:

> I call you to love me with all your heart, mind, soul and strength.
> You are to love me by obeying my Word.
> You are to love me by being willing to follow the leading of my Holy Spirit at all times.
> You are to love me by maintaining your relationship with me in faithful prayer.
> You are to love me by being a praising people.

You are to love me by acknowledging my sovereignty and lordship over every aspect of your lives.
You are to love me by your willingness to serve me in any way that I choose.
You are to love me by accepting my authority in the community of which I call you to be a part.

You are to love your neighbour by fulfilling faithfully the ministries and responsibilities I give you as part of the community;
by devoting yourself to the cause of my Kingdom, to bring new life, faith and healing to others.
You are to be faithful in your prayer for my Church and for this nation.
You are to be faithful in your prayer for revival and the moving of my Holy Spirit in the nations of the world.

You are to love one another as I have loved you.
This is to be expressed in the fellowship that you enjoy together.
You are to learn to live for one another;
You are to share all things in common.
You are to recognise that the family to which you belong encompasses all those whom I bring into this community.
You are not to seek to be independent nor to keep yourselves from fellowship with one another.
You are to allow my Spirit to lead you into these relationships which will be a true expression of my love.

You are to entrust yourselves to me to be your Father who cares for you and provides for you. You are to believe that I will be faithful and true to my Word and my promises. You are to live by faith in me, depending upon my love and grace.

You are to trust one another as fellow brothers and sisters of the covenant that I make with you. You are to agree to love, care for, encourage and support one another in fulfilling this covenant.

Know that I shall be true in pouring out my abundant riches upon you.

Understand that this is an expression of the eternal covenant you have in my Son, Jesus. Every time you celebrate the feast of His body and blood you are to remember this covenant.

The test of love

The Kingdom Faith leadership hope that in time many families will begin to open up their homes to provide respite and healing for those in need. When, for example, a drug addict has been set free or someone is coming to terms with past abuse, the ministry they have received will need to be consolidated. The ideal, believes Colin, is for such care to be available in every local church, perhaps removing the need for special institutions of this nature.

God, of course, sees the heart behind the service to others. What also matters to Him is the way we treat each other. Colin explains that most New Testament teaching on submission emphasises that we must be submitted *to one another*:

'Finally, all of you, live in harmony with one another; be sympathetic, love as brothers, be compassionate and humble. Do not repay evil with evil or insult with insult, but with blessing, because to this you were called so that you may inherit a blessing. For,

> 'Whoever would love life
> and see good days
> must keep his tongue from evil
> and his lips from deceitful speech.
> He must turn from evil and do good;
> he must seek peace and pursue it.
> For the eyes of the Lord are on the righteous
> and His ears are attentive to their prayer,
> but the face of the Lord is against those who do evil.'
> (1 Peter 3:8–12)

The implication of verses 8–9 is that the way you treat one another affects what you inherit.

'Submit to one another out of reverence for Christ.' (Ephesians 5:21)

In other words, if I do *not* submit to others, I do *not* have reverence for Christ.

This teaching affects the way a group of believers relates to each other and the way they do their jobs; such harmony is vital in a community of any sort, as Colin has discovered:

'If everyone within a body functions as they are called, the body will function as God intends. It's not love or submission to one another if you decide to do another job which you think you're better at than the one called to do it. What follows puts a strain on others when they have to do your job for you.'

Loving your neighbour in practical ways also constitutes the unwritten curriculum which distinguishes Kingdom Faith students' courses from more conventional theological studies.

Kingdom Faith students learn how to love in a very practical way; at regular intervals they sweep, mop, dust, vacuum, serve food and wash up.

Colin has never had a job which is not practical in some way; any idea that serving God took place in an ivory tower vanished with his first job as a curate. His vicar, a hard taskmaster, expected him to work from 7 a.m. to 10 p.m. Most of his courting of Caroline had to take place between 10 p.m. and midnight!

The Kingdom Faith leadership believe that practical work is as vital a preparation for ministry as prayer and Bible study. John McKay points to all the overseas students who have returned home to set up their own 'Roffey Places'. At one such place in India, the students sleep, eat and study in a single large room, rolling up their mattresses each morning before work begins.

Obviously ministry in Britain involves serving others in a practical way too, frequently because there are not the funds to employ domestic staff. At the end of a long Saturday conducting weddings in his first job, Colin asked his vicar who swept up all the confetti littering the church steps. His boss looked him straight in the eye and replied: 'You do.'

Colin tells how he started sweeping up the confetti, grumbling all the while to God: 'Lord' (sweep), 'did I spend four years' (sweep) 'in theological college' (sweep) 'just to clear up confetti?'

And God replied, 'Yes, you did.'

Now Colin still empties his own rubbish and frequently preaches against the 'super-spiritual' who attend all the prayer meetings but fail to make sufficient practical contribution to communal life. Caroline, too, has had plenty of girls move into her household who were very good at going off to pray but less eager to help clean.

The advantage of living close to one another is that such behaviour cannot last long: as one Anglican vicar wrote home during his sabbatical term at Roffey Place, 'If you know someone's not cleaning the bathroom, you're not going to pay much attention to what they say in a meeting.' After this was reported in his church magazine, he heard that parishioners were almost queuing up to clean his church's lavatories.

Serving in the kitchen is definitely an opportunity for Bible students to 'die to themselves'. As one put it, 'If you're learning to serve, especially in the kitchen when it's hot and sticky, that's when you need to realise you've died to self.'

The kitchen is recognised as the flashpoint for tensions. 'It's always in the kitchen that people's problems show up,' said a team member.

In fact, the deciding factor for Colin when considering someone for the team is whether or not they are helpful in the kitchen.

'Change comes from being submitted to God,' said the same person. 'If you don't want to change, you won't.'

While the atmosphere at Roffey seems peaceful to the outsider, thanks to the presence of God's Spirit, it can also be a place of great inner turmoil as people, especially new students, meet with God in a closer way than ever before. It has been described as a crucible or 'spiritual hothouse', for in term time there are up to ninety people (with plans to accommodate more students) living in a confined space and obliged to relate closely to each other all day and every day. Such close contact inevitably causes people to have to face up to less pleasant aspects of their own and others' characters sooner rather than later. It is not for nothing that Colin talks about the 'sandpaper ministry' of unlikely personalities rubbing up against each other; whereas most Christians who live in a small household and attend a local church or fellowship usually find they are able to keep those with whom they have less in common at arm's length, in a community this is not possible.

'You've got to face these things in yourself, or you have to retreat completely,' says Guy Barton. And students are not encouraged to isolate themselves – that is not what their course is about. Hiding in the library, in one's bedroom or the TV lounge is possible, but the student who does so soon recognises that they are missing out on what God is doing amongst the others. Guy finds the memory amusing: 'Occasionally you see someone at Roffey trying to retreat, but they don't usually last long before they have to come out again because it's unbearable! Not only are you missing out on the life, but quite apart from that several people come chasing after you because they realise what you're doing and they want to relate to you . . .'

The key benefit of living with other believers should be the freedom to grow by making mistakes. For this reason Colin emphasises the importance of not judging and criticising:

'The last thing people want to hear is that they're wrong when they know they are. The Bible tells us to encourage one another.'

The combination of encouragement while living in repentance before God means people's hearts are open.

'There was a very genuine unity and love amongst the Bethany Fellowship,' remembered Charles Sibthorpe. 'When there were problems, we knew we just needed time to get before the Lord. I'd bring the team together so we could open our hearts to Him. While we were worshipping, people would cross the room to apologise to others for being a pain and seek their forgiveness. Things were usually resolved in an hour or so, rather than sitting around discussing why one person knowingly hassled someone else last Tuesday.'

Having since experienced the tensions within other ministry organisations, Charles believes that it was God who produced the unity and commitment to each other at that time.

Love, however strong, functions better within a framework. Communities and extended households must have rules for everyone's comfort. Caroline Urquhart found that although everything more or less worked out in a small extended household, more organisation became necessary as the numbers increased. 'We allocated responsibilities to people for different areas of housework and cooking. We did it that way to avoid the stairs being washed down four times a week!'

A danger of community life is that it can breed irresponsibility, especially amongst the young. When everything belongs to everyone in general and no one in particular, there is a tendency to expect 'someone else' to have taken responsibility for looking after communal items. Michael Barling remembers that a car he had brought to The Hyde for communal use was ruined when it ran dry – no one had thought to put water in it.

Household contents were common property, so when the Barlings joined the Bethany Fellowship, they did not expect to keep the contents of their former London home together.

'The fridge went in one direction, the cooker in another direction, according to other people's needs at the time.'

For some years before knowing Colin, Michael was very committed to living within a community, particularly in an extended family. To this day he and his wife June usually have a younger, single person living in their house.

An open, caring home was the ideal for Michael and Colin's families, and moving into The Hyde was part of the Barlings' commitment to the vision.

With two families living in one house, however, the dining arrangements at The Hyde meant that everyone had meals together and opportunities for training one's own children were limited. Caroline stipulated that the children should help wash up after the evening meal, but it did not always work out like that. After meals the adults were so keen to show their Christian love for one another that about 50 per cent of them headed for the washing up. That meant that the children were often nowhere to be seen.

Francis Pym and his wife Marigold were part of the community at The Hyde from 1979 to 1986 with their four children. Living in a community was 'very much on their agenda' as they had been used to people living with them for several years previously.

'When we first got there, it was a very small team of just about six or seven people,' Marigold remembers. 'Then we joined, with the Sibthorpes and David Brown, and it ended up with stacks and stacks of us all living in one house.

'The whole experience of living in that community changed my life and taught me about faith – real faith. We'd literally just begun to get into healing and gifts of the Spirit before that.'

The commitment to one another at The Hyde was absolute. 'We all had to give up the right to quit,' recalls Marigold. 'You were there for the duration – or until the Lord moved you on. The commitment was intense, and it was all so exciting that no-one ever wanted to go away on holiday, in case something happened, which it invariably did. We didn't want to miss *anything*.'

The word which sums up the benefits of a close-knit community is 'bonding'. When a Kingdom Faith team member gets married, the food, photography and flowers will all be provided by college and church members. Barbara Redmore, who married Nick, a fellow team member in 1992, was particularly touched when she was even given the extra money needed for a going-away outfit, the one item she could not afford.

Elizabeth Scofield, who was connected to the Bethany Fellowship, although not living in The Hyde itself, still feels extraordinarily close to members of that fellowship whenever she meets them, even after a gap of several years. 'Our commitment to one another bonded us; God just gave us a sense of belonging.'

There seemed no limit to what fellowship members would do for each other. Elizabeth recalls many little kindnesses, such as Francis Pym driving out to their house in the depths of snowy winter to see how they were managing. She felt she could never do enough for others in return, even though she housed another family for several years. 'They were only going to stay for a few months, but in the end they arrived with two children and left with four!'

Part of living in community involves sacrifice of privacy and personal space. When Francis and Marigold left a big house in Yorkshire to move to The Hyde they felt it very proper that they and their four children should be accommodated in just two large rooms. Their children became part of a crowd of children there: 'As well as our four, Colin had three, another family had five – there were masses of children. I remember on one occasion these children formed a kind of crocodile, marching through our room, over our bed, through the next room, over the beds of all the children and out the other side. The next day Colin's teaching began: "Now what you must do is learn to live in love and forgiveness with everybody"!'

The size of Francis and Marigold Pym's vision, and that of many others, was expanded when they saw what God could do amongst a small group of people submitted to Him and committed to one another. The Bethany Fellowship at The Hyde provided the model for them and many others and led to their becoming more spiritually ambitious with a positive appetite to see what God would do, if truly welcomed, amongst His people.

The Urquhart children have little memory of not living in an extended family. When Clive was just six, he heard a commotion in the front garden one day and looked out of the window. Some children he had never seen before were playing with the toys he had left outside. Going to Caroline, he asked, 'Mum, what are those children doing here?'

'They're coming to live with us,' he was told.

In subsequent years when the Urquhart family had ministry colleagues living with them, Caroline ensured that family life was kept intact as far as possible; certainly she stipulates that talk about work does not dominate mealtimes.

In fact none of the Urquhart, Barling or Sibthorpe children went 'off the rails' and all are now strong Christians. Clive Urquhart, his street credibility enhanced by a ponytail, runs the fast-growing Kingdom Faith Church youth group and plays the drums in the worship team; he has a secure enough relationship with his father to retort from behind his drums when Colin makes jokes about his hair length in front of three hundred people. After growing up in a shared home, he was praying with his wife Jane for a big house of their own which they could open up to others. Their prayer was answered in 1992 when Colin and Caroline moved to their own house in Crawley and left Clive and Jane to take over the running of the big family house at Roffey Place. Andrea Urquhart has been in charge of the three- to four-year-olds' work at Faith Camp during her university vacations while her sister Claire, like Caroline, is a happily married full-time mother.

At The Hyde there were, for almost all of the time, two households grouped around two families in order to preserve the sense of a family unit. Each family had its own bedrooms, sitting-room and bathroom, although the building's facilities required that mealtimes were shared.

At the time it was an interesting and generally successful experiment, although some, like Michael Barling, would have preferred to have mealtimes with their own family. Michael believes the nuclear family is a God-given unit which should be open to becoming an extended family to single or wounded people who need a sense of family.

'If there is the room, the maximum number of singles living with you should be three – two guys and a girl, or vice versa.'

After various experiences of his own, he issues a challenge to local churches to be more caring, citing his mother-in-law's lonely illness after she had been part of a 'successful' London church for many years.

Extended households certainly have a place in the vision for revival, as a natural consequence of a church's desire to be a real family. As Colin said, 'Jesus didn't talk much about love – He just did it! He didn't put His arm round people and say, "There, there, God loves you." Praise God He didn't behave like a Christian!'

Chapter Five

HOLINESS: GOD'S MOST DESIRABLE GIFT

'Because you are holy I want you to live a holy life.

'Oh, there we go again. Fear! This fear is very deeply ingrained in you, isn't it? Every time I tell you that I expect holiness in your life you get very fearful. Let me ask you a question. Who lived the holy life, I mean a perfect holy life? That's right – Jesus. Was he miserable? No! The anointing of joy upon him raised him above his companions. Was he fearful, depressing or legalistic? Did he restrict people so much that they avoided his presence? No! Only the traditionalists wanted to avoid him because they were content with a formal kind of religion. Those who recognised their need were attracted by his holiness.'[1]

Colin is aware that holiness is not at the top of many Christians' list of desires, but it has become a key part of his teaching.

For years he has been convinced that personal holiness is the key to revival: 'The nation will have revival when it sees a holy body of people. The Church is weak because people think they're doing enough to keep God happy.'

Without holiness we may experience renewal and excitement, but not revival. Lack of holiness certainly helps explain why the charismatic renewal has blessed churches and even been investigated by the press and television as a spiritual phenomenon but has failed to be phenomenal enough to have an impact on the nation.

Colin believes God is saying to His people, 'I will change the nations when I've changed *you*.'

The words which God spoke to the Jews thousands of years ago are prophetic for Britain and other countries today:

'I will show the holiness of my great name, which has been profaned among the nations, the name you have profaned among them. Then the nations will know that I am the Lord, . . . *when I show myself holy through you before their eyes.*' (Ezekiel 36:23) (italics mine)

To show Himself through His people, God has to cleanse them first:

> 'I will sprinkle clean water on you, and you will be clean; I will cleanse you from all your impurities and from all your idols. I will give you a new heart and put a new spirit in you; I will remove from you your heart of stone and give you a heart of flesh. And I will put my Spirit in you and move you to follow my decrees and be careful to keep my laws. You will live in the land I gave your forefathers; you will be my people, and I will be your God.' (Ezekiel 36:25–28)

This is God's way of reviving His people, and anyone yearning for revival, weary of impurities and idols not only in the nation around them but in their own and other Christians' lives, can thrill to these promises while making them their prayer.

Holiness is to be the hallmark of the Christian's life, a consecration of thought, word and deed which will affect all those around him, as he lives out the words of the choruses he joyfully sings on Sunday mornings.

People who are drawn to Kingdom Faith Church or Bible College by its reputation as a place of God's presence, soon learn that the holiness God requires of them does not stop at the door of the worship hall, as Colin explains:

'We can all say the right things in the prayer meeting but we must learn to say them in the corridor. We can all say the right things to someone's face – but we must learn to say them behind their back, too. We think they're little things, but to God they're big. So be obedient in the little things and He'll put you in charge of big things.

'It's not enough for any of us to say, "I've made my big decision – and yes, there may be some criticism or gossip here and a bit of sin under the carpet there, but all my life belongs to you, Lord."'

Many Christians today want to see the Holy Spirit's power at work, but fear that being holy twenty-four hours a day is an impossible task. This was especially the case for David Hazeldine, who admits that his past times of reading his Bible, praying and listening to God had not been particularly exciting. 'TV and sport appealed to me more because they were more exciting. I knew holiness was right, because the Bible says you can't see the Lord without holiness, and the pure in heart are blessed because they will see God. But I wasn't totally convinced I wanted a pure heart because that meant getting rid of all the things in the world!'

He asked God whether his suspicions were correct. The Lord told him, 'You're judging holiness by fleshly, human standards – what *you* can make it be. You're thinking the future is going to be like the past – but it won't be if you're walking with Me.'

This was corroborated for David by the scripture, 'His compassions . . . are new every morning'. (Lamentations 3:22,23)

'So every time you come into God's presence there's something new. And He's brought me to a stage where I've experienced His presence coming into the room a couple of times when I've been worshipping. It hasn't been so great an awareness that I've fallen to the ground, but I've been more aware He was there than just having a sense in my mind.'

David is one of many who has become aware that holiness means complete obedience to God's commands: 'God showed me that my time wasn't my time; He bought me for a price, by the blood of Jesus, so all my time is His.

'And if He's Lord, that means He's Lord when He desires, not when I desire. So His time isn't just from 6 o'clock till 8 o'clock in the morning, it's *all* the time, including when I'm working and especially at the end of the day. When I finish work at 5.30 p.m. I'm absolutely shattered after gardening all day and I just want to sit down in front of the TV. But then you feel the tug of the Holy Spirit to pray and come aside and be with the Lord or feast on the word.'

For David, this was holiness – preferring to be with the Lord than watch television or chat to friends.

In turn he has become more aware of Christ's passion and tenderness for His people and is learning how to repay some of it. He quotes the verse in Song of Songs which says, 'I belong to my lover and he desires me.'

'This means I belong to Jesus first of all, not anybody else. He desires me so as He's got my time He can call upon me at any time because I belong to Him – I want to belong to Him so I have to obey Him. If He wakes me up in the middle of the night, then I know I've got to pray. Sometimes He's woken me up in quite strange circumstances and even before I've got out of bed to pray, He's told me people He'd like me to pray about. So I've spent up to an hour just worshipping and praying about people, with revelations He's given me.'

He points out, though, that dedication to God does not mean losing touch with the outside world – he still keeps in touch by listening to the news. Perhaps his most important revelation was that holiness was not something he could successfully manufacture; it was born out of his love relationship with Jesus, and his desire to be holy is there because he let the Lord put it there.

Such breakthroughs have been achieved by many during regular weeks of 'revival' meetings, begun in 1992, which God prompted Colin to launch in order for the college and church to experience personal revival. The emphasis of those meetings was one of consecration and personal holiness.

The call to holiness

The third series of 'revival' meetings in October 1992 saw the first glimmering of God's reviving power which became a landmark in the ministry's history. At the same time, many had a breakthrough into personal revival. The turning point came on the third night of meetings, when many expressed a fresh desire for holiness; having cleared out a fair amount of debris, they had a deeper desire to obey Jesus' commands.

By now most people recognised that holiness was next to godliness, which simply meant having more of Jesus in your life; in other words, 'life in abundance' rather than the false idea of deprivation. It had taken a few months, however, for everyone to receive this revelation! When Colin had first told the team and students that we needed to meet with God in His holiness and become more holy ourselves, the reaction was not one of loud 'Hallelujahs'. Colin was amused: 'You look as though I've asked you to give up eating.'

Rather like virtue, the idea of holiness is one which I had assumed automatically came as part of the package of being a Christian. Surely it followed on – a sort of by-product of loving and following Jesus?

It was not as simple as that. Step one was repentance – perhaps on a deeper level than one had known before. It was more than saying 'sorry' to God for all the sins one could think of; we asked the Holy Spirit to show us all those areas in which we were not loving God (or each other). After confessing them in prayer meetings or to another person (James 5:16), we experienced a new awareness of and aversion to all the ungodly attitudes and traits which we had previously dismissed as 'the way I'm made'.

Giving up a small amount of eating did in fact play a part in the team's consecration. In the two weeks before the revival meetings, the team and students fasted lunch in order to devote the lunch hour to a prayer meeting. For some of us, this was more of a sacrifice than for others! At one of the early meetings we were asked to pray with whoever was nearest for their heart's desire. The nearest person to me was a young man from another church who announced he wanted God to give him more anointing. I looked at him comfortably filling out his denim jacket and rather irritably thought, 'You can't just waltz in here looking for more anointing – I've gone without lunch for two weeks and I'm still going through basic obedience classes with God. I'm still learning to respond to simple commands like sit – stay – pray!'

None too graciously I muttered to him something about all the repentance we had had to go through, trying to imply that anointing didn't always arrive like manna from heaven. He listened, smiling happily, while I stumbled through a less than anointed prayer before he prayed vigorously for my heart's desire at the time – a car . . .

Later I went and apologised to him, once the Holy Spirit had reminded me that my attitude had been unloving.

Happily, the third revival week I experienced saw a change in me; I actually wanted God to move into my life to a greater extent because the fear of having sin exposed had gone. This time I welcomed the time of preparation, in the same way that many of the team looked forward to the first week of term. That was another week for clearing out debris and sometimes became a baptism of fire for new students. Its official name was 'Seeking the Lord week', but amongst some of the students it became fondly known as 'Bite the carpet time', due to periods when some chose to lie on their faces before God. As Colin said, 'There may be a few tears, but then you can rejoice that you're purified.'

Many Christians struggle with a sense of guilt and failure, often because they are not convinced their sins have been forgiven. Colin once made his listeners laugh when he pointed out that they highlighted in their Bibles those verses they found hardest to believe. Sure enough, almost everyone present had Romans 8:1–2 neatly outlined in pink, yellow or green:

'Therefore, there is now no condemnation for those who are in Christ Jesus, because through Christ Jesus the law of the Spirit of life set me free from the law of sin and death.'

In times of revival, doubt and guilt are swept away, sometimes dramatically. It is revival's holy paradox; the awareness of all that could give rise to doubt and guilt increases sharply, but it is followed by a total repentance which leaves the confesser convinced that the sin is left at the cross forever.

Open confession of sin is a feature of revival. Colin warns people to keep short accounts with God:

'When revival comes, you won't even dare think a wrong thought about anyone because you'll find yourself confessing it five minutes later!'

Living in the light

'Living in the light' (a reference to walking in the light, 1 John 1:7) was a popular phrase during and after the 1981 revival at The Hyde. Essentially it meant conducting one's life with complete openness, aiming always to be in that place of total righteousness with God and man. Unconfessed sin is a stumbling-block to peace, forgiveness and healing, so although initially daunting it is far easier to confess sin to each other (James 5:16), forgive others (unforgiveness is a sin) and receive the peace of God's forgiveness.

The breakthrough which set the pattern at The Hyde came on 2nd May 1981 when the presence of God swept majestically into the room. Everyone present fell to their knees and faces, crying out to God in repentance.

Consciousness of self vanished, another mark of revival which Colin longs for: 'You're totally given over to God. No one's looking round or contemplating their spiritual navel and thinking what a mess they are; you're just taken over by God's presence.'

God did 'a deep and powerful work' in the hearts of Charles and Joyce Sibthorpe at the time, breaking down the shells of convention with which they protected themselves. 'The conviction of sin was so strong that people were *compelled* to confess their sin,' said Joyce. 'It was a sovereign move of God which resulted in people crying out for forgiveness.'

One girl sobbed out her heart to God in such a vulnerable way that it had a 'knock-on effect and resulted in everybody just tipping things out'.

A man who had always seemed rather restricted before God received a vision reminding him of his previous contact with freemasonry. After confessing this he was a different person. The notable aspect was that he repented as a result of God dealing with him directly rather than in response to a word of knowledge.

Annette Callaway also had a strong exterior, giving the impression that 'everything was fine and I was nice'. Soon she realised that she was not quite as nice as she had thought and needed to let other people know about it. 'Once I started letting people see the real me, I realised that everybody else was just the same! Of course you could feel embarrassed after blurting out your sin in front of people, even if you knew them well, but you knew their turn was coming tomorrow!'

The community had already worked through 'Finney's list' (see page 97), a comprehensive list of Christians' most likely sins drawn up by the great revivalist Charles Finney; now they were opening up deeper levels of themselves to God, and He was dealing with areas which had not been healed or properly repented of yet, as well as sinful attitudes which many had not realised were grieving the Holy Spirit.

Joyce was suddenly shown that she was guilty of despising one of the leaders' lack of biblical knowledge. Although she knew the man was probably wary of her, she was not aware of deliberately making him feel awkward. All at once the lack of charity in her heart had been exposed: 'I saw clearly how I'd despised him and put him under pressure. The root of it was pride, and the Holy Spirit just cleansed that whole area. The Lord told me to humble myself and seek the man's forgiveness.'

The emphasis was not, Joyce found, on 'hearing everybody's grot come out', but on rejoicing as they were liberated.

The new dynamic created by the revival meant that visitors were affected too. Just before a mission to Wales, two men from the host church had come to spend a weekend of preparation at The Hyde. After some worship and teaching from Colin during a morning meeting, one of the women in the fellowship fell to the ground, pleading with God and crying. Her friend next to her was taken aback but prepared to stay in her place until she too found herself on the floor, crying out to God for forgiveness. The Holy Spirit had convicted her of something she had not known was within her. She was thinking to herself, 'Wait a minute, you don't usually do this,' when the two visitors beside her were thrown to the floor also. In tears, they confessed their sins.

They discovered the difference between routine repentance and what the fellowship knew as 'revival repentance'. In routine repentance all sorts of wrong thoughts may come to mind and be confessed, but they may be the same wrong attitudes for which you sought forgiveness a day or so earlier. In 'revival repentance' the Holy Spirit does the work of bringing conviction without the need for soul-searching. The conviction comes so swiftly that the effect can be devastating, but satisfying. It is irreversible.

'All I wanted to do was confess it and get it out,' remembers one of the fellowship. 'And afterwards I had a tremendous lightness in my spirit, and I just knew that that really wouldn't come back to trouble me again. That's one of the reasons revival is life-changing.'

It was this experience of 'revival repentance', the consequence of a new-found awareness of sin, with its echoes of the Welsh revival (amongst others), that the two men were then able to take back to their church. The subsequent mission in Wales saw a powerful move of God.

Brokenness

Another popular word used at the time was 'brokenness'. When Colin said 'There is no revival without holiness', he added, 'and no holiness without brokenness'.

To quote Charles Sibthorpe, who led The Hyde's leaders' weeks, 'Many people think that (brokenness) is to be so demoralised before God that you collapse in a heap of discouragement. What a lie of the enemy! Brokenness deals with your selfishness and pride so that the life of Jesus is liberated within you.'[2]

Holiness and the desire to please God come easily when one has had a powerful experience of the awesome nature of God's holiness. Pleasing God comes less easily when, for whatever reason, we have drifted away from Him. But if we believe Paul's words in Hebrews, we should always be dwelling in God's inner sanctuary:

> 'Therefore, brothers, since we have confidence to enter the Most Holy Place by the blood of Jesus, by a new and living way opened for us through the curtain, that is, his body, and since we have a great priest over the house of God, let us draw near to God with a sincere heart in full assurance of faith, having our hearts sprinkled to cleanse us from a guilty conscience and having our bodies washed with pure water.' (Hebrews 10:19–22)

God wants us to know how to stay in the inner sanctuary and not keep going in and out. We have to achieve this by faith, believing every moment of every day that we are in Christ and have His righteousness. According to Dan Chesney, too many Christians think they are still sinners – they have not had the revelation that they have been freed from sin. They may know it intellectually but remain unconvinced in their spirits.

How do we convince ourselves? By going over the basic tenets of our faith. We are all born into sin, because after the Fall sin corrupted all mankind, then spread into nature with weeds and pollution resulting! Paul makes it quite clear that sin entered the world through man – God did not cause or send it, so man must bear the responsibility of what happened:

'Therefore, just as sin entered the world through one man, and death through sin, and in this way death came to all men, because all sinned . . .' (Romans 5:12)

Nor are any of us guiltless before we acknowledge Jesus as our Saviour:

'All have sinned, and fall short of the glory of God.' (Romans 3:23)

Jesus' death on a cross has so many implications for our lives, that it can take years to appreciate and fully enter into the abundance purchased so dearly for us. One of the keys to 'life in all its fullness' for Colin was the discovery that he was 'dead'.

> 'For we know that our old self was crucified with him

> so that the body of sin might be done away with, that we should no longer be slaves to sin – *because anyone who has died has been freed from sin.*' (Romans 6:6–7) (italics mine)

Once we truly believe that our 'self' life is dead, we become aware of our new spiritual status.

> 'Your old self was crucified with Christ. The "body of sin" has been rendered powerless and no longer needs to control your life . . . Remember that sin itself still exists and there will always be the temptation to sin. But you do not need to yield to that temptation. You can count yourself dead to sin and alive in Christ, able to live His new life for His glory.'[3]

Counting oneself dead is something which might take practice. We understand, by faith, the fact of our 'death' with Christ, but then need to live out that spiritual truth. In Paul's letter to the Colossians he is taking them through this process, telling them to 'put to death' all the sins which were part of their earthly nature: '. . . you have taken off your old self with its practices and have put on the new self, which is being renewed in knowledge in the image of its Creator.' (Colossians 3:9–10)

Now they must 'clothe' themselves with compassion, kindness, humility, gentleness and patience. This simple illustration of taking off the old habits and putting on the new qualities can be a daily, even hourly, practice. Rather than struggle to be holy, we can simply confess our sins and know that in Christ we are purified from all unrighteousness.

'Death to self' is liberating, because we are set free from 'the basic principles of this world' (Colossians 2:20), which are all concerned with survival of the self: self-concern, self-pity, self-effort, self-consciousness, selfishness, self-adulation.

Once we accept that the self, our 'flesh life', counts for nothing, there is no need to be concerned with what others think of us. Wanting our abilities to be recognised can prevent our knowing peace and unity with God.

'God showed what he thought of your self by crucifying it!' explains Colin. 'So don't waste time defending your self; ask God to break down that wall of protection you've put round it because you thought it was still worth preserving!'

That wall of protection comes down in repentance. A few more bricks might be put in place whenever we give our 'selves' any importance, which shows our need for a life of repentance and brokenness before God.

Dan teaches that self-consciousness can make you disobedient to Jesus, a factor which prevents many talking openly about their faith:

'Once you've killed that self life, people's looks, sneers and innuendoes won't dampen your spirit. If you find you feel yucky and sinful, repent – but in faith! There's no point in repenting of vague things – that's an empty prayer. Ask the Holy Spirit to show you specific sins, ask God's forgiveness and then believe that you are forgiven.'

> 'I am not ashamed of the gospel, because it is the power of God for the salvation of everyone who believes: first for the Jew, then for the Gentile. For in the gospel a righteousness from God is revealed, *a righteousness that is by faith from first to last*, just as it is written: "The righteous will live by faith."' (Romans 1:16–17) (italics mine)

According to Colin, the biggest hindrance to holiness is unbelief.

'Any Christian who puts themselves down is acting in unbelief, unaware that they are just as free from sin as Jesus was.'

It is not what we do, but what we believe that makes us righteous. Righteousness gives us the power to resist sin on a daily basis, enabling us to believe that God is for us. It should not be a struggle to be righteous, rather we need to actively accept and thank God for what He has *already* done for us, each time we are tempted to look at ourselves and feel discouraged at the ways in which we are not fully expressing the life of Jesus.

'There's no faster way of getting depressed than by looking at the old ratbag of yourself! So keep your eyes fixed on Jesus and remind the enemy that you're a new creation because Christ is in you.'

Although it can seem introspective to concentrate on our personal level of holiness, its importance was one of the lessons learned in the ministry's last revival period. Colin admits it can seem nit-picking to be concerned with sins like criticism, jealousy and self-indulgence, but insists that in God's eyes it taints all the other work the Christian is doing for Him and actually hinders its fruitfulness.

'You cannot separate the righteousness that the Spirit desires to create in you from the joy and peace the believer wants to experience, or the signs and wonders you need to see. The Lord wants the total life and ministry of His Spirit to be evidenced in your life.'[4]

Elizabeth Allan remembers that love and holiness were Colin's themes during her time as a student.

'He was away travelling quite a lot of that time, but as soon as he came into the building there was this terrific atmosphere of holiness, a reflection of his personal walk with the Lord. However close I was to God, I became intensely aware of the distance between God's perfect holiness and the state of my heart. This led to further times of deep repentance over issues I had previously been unaware of or would have thought trivial.

For Colin, each time of repentance brings more fruit, although he would prefer to be on the mountain-top permanently!

'God graciously takes you higher than you could ever take yourself, but it's up to you to stay there. If you fall, you have to walk back up, which can take months or years!'

Evangelism is also hindered when holiness in Christians' personal lives is absent or diminished. Kevin Callaway, Kingdom Faith's evangelism director, described how a particular outreach was scuppered because he and his wife were not getting on well at that time. Similarly Dan Chesney knows he cannot get up and preach to people if there is anything wrong between him and someone else, particularly if that 'someone' is his wife with whom he has had a mild disagreement!

Helena Croft, Colin's secretary, also discovered that God was looking at the heart behind the words and deeds:

'Having the right heart attitude is a form of prayer. If you're being faithful in that way, it makes the rest of your prayer times so much easier because you're in the flow of the Spirit. It's not so much what you say – it's the communication between you and Him.'

Holiness is not an elusive concept which is beyond us – rather it is what God has made us in His sight, although, like our salvation, it is still being worked out.

When we have the revelation of who we are in Christ, we can live in the good of that.

Living in holiness produces powerful results, as Jesus proved when He fulfilled Isaiah's prophecy:

'Then will the eyes of the blind be opened
  and the ears of the deaf unstopped.
Then will the lame leap like a deer,
  and the mute tongue shout for joy.
Water will gush forth in the wilderness
  and streams in the desert.
The burning sand will become a pool,
  the thirsty ground bubbling springs.
In the haunts where jackals once lay,
  grass and reeds and papyrus will grow.
And a highway will be there;
  it will be called the Way of Holiness.
The unclean will not journey on it;
  it will be for those who walk in that Way;
  wicked fools will not go about on it.
(Isaiah 35:5–8)

The reference to streams in the desert is frequently used in prayer meetings when revival is sought. Jesus has established the Way of Holiness which is available to us, His disciples, today. We too should long to see blind eyes opened, deaf ears unstopped and cripples leaping, in both the spiritual and physical senses. Holiness, being in the right place before God, is the key.

> 'I am a stranger on earth;
>   do not hide your commands from me.
> My soul is consumed with longing
>   for your laws at all times.' (Psalm 119:19–20)

Finney's list: Preparing for Revival

Father, please search my heart by your Holy Spirit and reveal to me everything that hinders your purpose for me and among us as your people, in the name of Jesus and for His sake. Amen.

Examine your heart in detail concerning:

Brotherly love – relationships and attitudes towards others.
Dissension to authority.
Jealousy.
Speaking evil of others.
Worldliness.
Secret sins.
Laxity in spiritual discipline.
Unreliability
Hardness of heart – especially towards the Word.
Unholiness.
Lack of openness towards others.
Avoiding cost.

Ingratitude.
Want of love to God.
Neglect of the Bible.
Unbelief.
Neglect of prayer.
Neglect of means of grace.

Manner of performing duties.
Want of love for souls of fellow men.
Want of care for overseas missions.
Neglect of family duties.
Neglect of watchfulness over your own life.
Neglect to watch over your brethren.
Neglect of self-denial.
Worldly-mindedness.
Pride.
Envy.
Censoriousness.
Slander.
Levity.
Lying.
Cheating.
Hypocrisy.
Robbing God.
Bad temper.
Hindering others from being useful.

Chapter Six

FAITH WORKING THROUGH LOVE

'If you preach faith in this country, you get crucified', Colin once said.

In fact, he teaches that faith is inseparable from holiness, but he has lost count of the number of conferences he has led where he has been warned beforehand that certain visitors have booked in solely to criticise and gather ammunition. In the end, however, most have been disarmed by the authority with which the message has been presented and the opposition has melted away. The authority comes from submission to God and a willingness to proclaim His word, whatever the cost.

Yet it was the revelation of faith in God's word, especially His promises, which has made certain men household names in the Christian world. Yonggi Cho in Korea, Ray McCauley in South Africa and Ulf Ekman in Sweden (amongst others) all received a revelation of faith for revival in their nations. In working towards that goal, their churches and personal ministries have mushroomed. Each man would attribute all the glory to God, saying that it is He who 'gave the increase', while they concentrated on proclaiming Jesus.

Ask and you will receive

Discovering the necessity for biblical faith was a milestone in Colin's life. It came when he took seriously the prayer promises of Jesus. Once one realises that Jesus is speaking to His modern-day disciples, not just to the historical twelve, they are astounding:

'Therefore I tell you, whatever you ask for in prayer,

> believe that you have received it, and it will be yours.' (Mark 11:24)
>
> 'If you remain in me and my words remain in you, ask whatever you wish, and it will be given you. This is to my Father's glory, that you bear much fruit, showing yourselves to be my disciples.' (John 15:7–8)
>
> 'Ask and you will receive, and your joy will be complete.' (John 16:24)
>
> 'Dear friends, if our hearts do not condemn us, we have confidence before God and receive from him anything we ask, because we obey his commands and do what pleases him.' (1 John 3:21–22)
>
> 'This is the confidence we have in approaching God: that if we ask anything according to his will, he hears us. And if we know that he hears us – whatever we ask – we know that we have what we asked of him.' (1 John 5:14–15)
>
> 'I tell you the truth, anyone who has faith in me will do what I have been doing. He will do even greater things than these, because I am going to the Father. And I will do whatever you ask in my name, so that the Son may bring glory to the Father. You may ask me for anything in my name, and I will do it.' (John 14:12–14)

Colin lives with these verses every day, because it is a constant challenge to him. Teaching on them, he insists that the phrase 'greater things' does not simply mean 'more things' because Jesus died young, but greater miracles.

In fact, Colin teaches students that Jesus wanted His disciples to learn to think in Kingdom terms – which meant with faith. Jesus would rebuke His disciples for their lack of faith, for the way they persisted in looking at the world through 'natural' eyes rather than the eyes of faith. When the multitudes had to be fed, the disciples had a natural response: 'We're in the desert – there's no bakery here and even if there was, we haven't any dough!'

We are brought up in a world where our senses control

what we believe, which is what we can see, touch and hear. God's truth is in another dimension altogether; the dimension of the Spirit. We confuse facts with truth:

'If someone can see a cancer tumour on an X-ray, that's a fact,' says Colin. 'But the truth – God's truth – is that by the stripes of Jesus you have been healed. It's not a question of saying the cancer doesn't exist – it does. That is the fact. But spiritual truth is able to change the facts. Every one of us has a choice – to believe a fact, which is natural, or the truth, which is supernatural. Facts can't change the truth, but the truth can change facts.'

Every day the Christian determined to live by faith will have a battle in his mind between the truth and the facts, in the same way that there is conflict between the flesh and the Spirit.

Knowing certain things would be hard to swallow, Jesus prefaced His most challenging phrases with 'I tell you the truth'.

Frequently the truth offends our reason, which many of us still want to place above God's truth, especially in difficult circumstances. Similarly we tend to believe our feelings above the truth, which means we are operating at the soul level.

Worship leader Carol Owen says: 'The main thing I've learned at Roffey is not to trust my feelings, but the word of God, and that Jesus has forgiven all my sins and healed all my diseases.'

Many 'mature' Christians have been persuaded by their experience that God's promises are somehow not for them. And Colin is not unsympathetic to their predicament, although he points out that God has never failed to answer the prayer of faith, 'even though our experience sometimes suggests otherwise'.

However, often Christians will go around saying, 'I'm believing God' for something and will not receive it – because they have not had a word from God about it.

Nor can we claim God's promises in the Bible for ourselves unless we fulfil the conditions attached to them. Jesus tells His disciples, 'If you remain in me and my words remain in you, ask whatever you wish, and it will be given you. This is to my Father's glory, that you bear much fruit, showing yourselves to be my disciples.' (John 15:7–8)

Colin teaches that there is both a condition and a purpose to this promise. The condition is to remain close to Jesus and the purpose is to produce fruit from doing His work. In addition, it is worth noting that the Greek for 'words' here is *rhema, the word for the moment*. It is not *logos*, the whole body of God's words. We know when we have received a *rhema* word from God: that word or section of scripture seems to be spotlit on the page and we re-read it several times as we absorb its meaning for our character or circumstances.

Hearing the Holy Spirit

We need to hear the Holy Spirit speaking to our spirits whenever we can; and the best way to activate this process is by studying, 'confessing' (proclaiming) and praying scripture. Some well-known lines from Proverbs proclaimed this truth thousands of years ago:

> 'My son, keep your father's commands
> and do not forsake your mother's teaching.
> Bind them upon your heart for ever;
> fasten them around your neck.
> When you walk, they will guide you;
> when you sleep, they will watch over you;
> when you awake, *they will speak to you*.'
> (Proverbs 6:20–22) (italics mine)

At The Hyde, Francis Pym derived 'tremendous benefit' from seeing the word of God actually wielded as the 'sword of the Spirit'. (Ephesians 6:17)

'Colin showed how speaking out the word of God, confessing it, knowing it, receiving it and particularly hearing it in one's spirit actually causes a change.'

Doing this brought about in his life not only the change spoken of in Hebrews 4:12, but also the ability to use the word of God as a weapon: 'For the word of God is living and active. Sharper than any double-edged sword, it penetrates even to dividing soul and spirit, joints and marrow; it judges the thoughts and attitudes of the heart.' (Hebrews 4:12)

Faith gets a bad name when some people use the Bible as a magic rule-book, striving for the effects without the cause. In other words, when *we* decide what we want, rather than asking God what *He* wants. Dan Chesney relates how God told him to conduct evangelistic crusades when he was first sent to England. So he nose-dived into evangelistic activity – and wondered why after nine crusades in two years he was exhausted and in debt. When he asked God for the explanation, he was told that he hadn't listened to further instruction as to how, where and when God wanted crusades to take place. God told him, 'The problem I have with you pastors and evangelists is that I give you the vision and then you go and do it your own way!'

Conversely there are plenty of Christians who do not believe they are special enough to God to warrant what they would see as favours. Or their experience might persuade them to believe that God's promises are only valid for one area of their lives. But His word holds as true for relationships as it does for healing and provision.

'Confessing' or speaking aloud God's word can be a wonderful aid to building up faith. Dan Chesney did it for a whole hour a day for two years and it still forms a regular part of his prayer life: 'Fear vanished – there was no room for it – and with such a foundation it's the first thing which comes out of my mouth in a crisis.'

If, as Dan believes, maintaining revival will owe as much to Christians in secular jobs as to full-time leaders, it is vital for all of us to be so schooled in Scripture that our reactions in crisis are those of faith! It need not be a crisis with national implications; domestic ones are quite sufficient to provoke ungodly reactions. With his fondness for homespun illustrations, Dan cities the case of the wife who drops her hot soufflé because one of the children has started screaming. Her husband comes in and tells her off for being careless while hot soufflé oozes over her shoe. What's her first reaction? Does she threaten murder or say 'I'm a forgiver!'?

'You will keep in perfect peace
him whose mind is steadfast,
because he trusts in you.' (Isaiah 26:3)

'God's word is your stabiliser,' says Dan. He warns us to expect what he ironically calls 'surprise exams' – tests of faith. For example, you go to the doctor for routine test results and are told to prepare for bad news. Is your reaction: 'Aargh! I'm going to die!' or 'By his stripes I am healed'?

Your reaction in this particular instance proves how necessary it is to be braced for healing *at all times*, so that ill health cannot catch you unawares. In the same way we have to train ourselves to believe in God's provision when we are well-off rather than waiting until we are in need. This training and schooling is part of the maturing of a Christian as he learns to act on God's word in everyday situations. Maturity will bring a stability to his life as he sees God's words changing the circumstances so he is able to rejoice rather than plunge into gloom at an apparent setback.

In Jesus' parable of the house built on rock (Matthew 7:24–27), the wise man builds his life on a foundation of God's word; when the storm strikes, it meets the solid rock of faith. The wise man not only heard the words of Jesus, but *put them into practice*, so even in life's storms he remains in perfect peace. As these verses affirm: '. . . the mind controlled by the Spirit is life and peace.' (Romans 8:6) 'God opposes the proud but gives grace to the humble.' (James 4:6)

In Scripture the 'proud' are also the self-centred. It's helpful, whenever looking at one of these scriptures which talks about behaviour, to look at the reverse meaning to get a better understanding of the true meaning.

For Colin, 'humility' isn't going around saying, 'I'm no good' – that's negative self-confidence. 'Submit yourselves, then, to God. Resist the devil, and he will flee from you.' (James 4:7)

As Colin explains, 'The immediate outcome of submission to God is that the devil flees! So next time you can't make something go away, look very carefully to see if you're *in true submission to God*. You can pray all the right things, but you won't have faith and conviction if you're not completely submitted to God – and this does *not* mean the negative prayer of unbelief, "Your will be done, Lord", i.e. "I'm only a passive passenger with no rights or authority"! Once submitted, start exercising your authority properly.'

Jesus has given us, His disciples, authority over *all* the power of the enemy. This extends to the weather! When Jesus was on the way to deliver the Gerasene demoniac (Mark 4:35–5:20), the storm which blew up was severe enough to frighten the disciples, who were experienced fishermen.

Logic dictates that this particular weather pattern was not from God – if it was, Jesus would not have rebuked the storm. A parallel example is that of sickness – if God had inflicted sickness on people, Jesus would not have healed them. Thus this storm came from the enemy; Satan knew that Jesus would deliver the demoniac from all the evil spirits he had inflicted on him.

Therefore the believer has authority over weather patterns clearly not in God's will. The weather pattern changed several times during Colin's ministry at Luton when believers stood in faith together. On one occasion Colin was on the way to speak about the Holy Spirit, when he and the team with him found they were in thick fog. Clearly they would not arrive on time for the meeting. They pulled into the side of the road, prayed briefly, and when they opened their eyes the fog had lifted. Similarly the team has always seen prayers answered for good weather at Kingdom Faith's annual Family Camp. In the area around Peterborough where it is held, the fine weather for that week of August has become something of a tradition. One year when the rest of the British Isles was being lashed by storms, the weatherman reported 'a halo of good weather over Peterborough'. Now the local weatherman predicts good weather for that week because it is the week of Faith Camp!

Almost every morning of the year except August, one of the Kingdom Faith leaders – usually Colin, John McKay or Michael Barling – speak to the team (and students in term-time) during their morning worship. It is an extraordinarily rich spiritual diet. Often team members can take it for granted – until they go elsewhere. Sometimes they return almost shaken after ministering in other places.

Faith working through love

Colin is keen that they should not take for granted the spiritual dynamic that exists at Roffey, but should ensure they are being built up in Christ. It would be possible, though difficult, to coast spiritually, ducking challenges and being carried along by the faith of others. He is unwilling that anyone should take for granted the basic provision they receive from the ministry for their everyday needs. As well as having faith that God, not Kingdom Faith, will meet their material needs, be it clothes, holidays or housing, he would like them to reach that place where they actively trust God for *all* their needs, although he recognises that people are at different stages of faith.

That has been the case with the new ministry base set up at Lamplugh House in Yorkshire. In November 1991 a group of young team members, led by the unassuming Bryan Spence, set off with a few vans full of furniture and possessions to start a new Christian training and conference centre. They had two months to prepare the base before the first students arrived.

Before they left, Colin made it clear to them that they should not look to the main base for support. 'You must have your own faith for housing,' he told them. 'I'm not an estate agent – I can't have faith for all of you as well as the ministry here.'

It undoubtedly helped the young team to know exactly where they were. They have been stretched spiritually and physically in adapting to a new home, a new set of relationships with each other and, in some cases, new job descriptions. Bryan was told by God to ask team members what jobs they had been told to do by the Holy Spirit. Each one fitted in perfectly with the needs of the centre.

With God's grace they became a cohesive team, living out their own dynamic of faith working through love. Many have been thrown into the deep end in terms of ministry, but have been helped by Bryan's gentle encouragement. An older team member, one of the very few who have been allowed to join without being a Kingdom Faith student first, said ruefully, 'I'd been counselling in my old church for twenty years, but it's still a shock when Bryan tells me I've got a word for a particular person in a meeting. It's even more of a shock when I see a nineteen-year-old confidently doing what I'm scared to try! But I'm gaining confidence all the time.'

Their faith was rewarded by miraculous provision just a year after opening, confirming that God would supply everything they needed if they were in His will. The building needed a major overhaul to be equipped for all the work they knew God wanted to happen there. Beginning with only £200 in the bank, Bryan committed workmen to the job. 'We had to get down and ask God for the money,' he said. 'But He provided for us in ways that repeatedly showed the tenderness of His love. One person gave us their life savings because they knew that was what God wanted.'

Within that first year over £45,000 was received, enabling the overhaul to be completed and paid for. The value of work carried out was greater, but several of the skilled workmen volunteered to work at reduced rates.

Colin sums up his belief that God will supply all the ministry's needs with Jesus' well-known words from the sermon on the mount:

'But seek first his kingdom and his righteousness, and all these things will be given to you as well.' (Matthew 6:33)

As long as Colin has been obedient to God's leading, provision has been forthcoming.

Unlike most sizable ministries, Kingdom Faith does not have a budget, a situation which would appall some leaders. Colin's explanation is simple: 'If we drew up a budget at the start of the year, we wouldn't be able to respond to all the Lord told us to do. And if we knew in advance what the Lord would tell us to do, we might be so horrified we'd pack our bags!'

Living in a community, however, means that provision should be dependent on other people's faith as well as

Colin's, a fact of life he wants all the team to realise. 'You must believe for yourselves,' he told them. 'I shouldn't have to have faith for all of you as well as for the ministry.'

This biblical interdependence is vulnerable to outside attack. Disobedience or unconfessed sin in the community affects everyone else, not only in financial provision. There was just one occasion at The Hyde when the cash flow dried up. Colin called the community together in prayer. The source of disobedience was revealed, repentance followed, and at once the gifts began to flow in again.

In the matter of personal giving and receiving, Colin is unequivocal, often repeating one of his favourite Kingdom principles: 'The measure you give is the measure you receive back.'

When he and Caroline were first married, they increased their giving year by year from 10 to 12 to 14 per cent and so on. They were aiming to be able to live on 10 per cent of their income. This has probably been achieved now, although impossible to quantify, because it is Colin's ministry which supports all the team at Kingdom Faith.

The purchase of Roffey Place summed up the necessity of praying with faith. It looked extremely unlikely that a group of guernsey-clad Christians living in community and holding all things in common would have the financial muscle to buy a newly-built, fully-equipped college. On paper they did not have the £600,000 required. Yet by faith they did, because they knew beyond doubt that it was God's revealed will for them to have it. In 1982 Colin had been praying one day when God spoke to him very clearly:

'I want you to believe *now* for that training college.'

Immediately he thought of some farm buildings on The Hyde estate which could have been turned into a college. It would be ideally placed to be positively affected by what was happening in the main house. But the buildings were unavailable at that time.

When Colin shared the Lord's communication with the other elders, they all felt, in their spirits, that it was right to seek premises for a college. Within a week, they heard that Roffey Place, a college attached to a house ten minutes away from The Hyde, was on the market. The ready-made teaching facility seemed almost too good to be true, and indeed the estate agents made it clear there was no point in looking over it: a sale had already been agreed.

Since contracts had not been exchanged, however, the elders insisted on seeing it. 'I think they thought we were a bit of a nuisance,' recalls Colin. 'So we came to see it and as we walked round, we were thinking how good it was – almost beyond anything we could have imagined. But we didn't have any money. Being a faith ministry, we just looked to the Lord for all our needs.'

Roffey Place's asking price was £600,000 minimum, which was worth far more in 1982 than it is now. As well as the potential buyer, several other businesses were interested in it. There was little the fellowship could do at the time, except say, 'Well, Lord, if this is the place, we believe that You will keep it.'

As the ministry was already believing God would supply the needs of other projects at the time, Roffey Place was put on the back burner for a few weeks. Then they heard that the agreed sale had fallen through. The estate agents phoned to say that the owners would be meeting the very next day to decide which of several offers they should accept. If the fellowship were still interested in Roffey Place, they had to make an offer within twenty-four hours and state the method of payment.

That day the eldership had a crisis meeting. Colin announced that God was telling them to offer £570,000: 'Never mind if they're only accepting offers of £600,000 plus; if God is in this, we're going to get it.'

After putting in the offer, they also had to offer a 'token' £10,000 for the contents as the college was fully equipped.

They offered to pay by cash, because that was how the ministry operated. After the owners' meeting, they discovered that their offer, not the highest by any means, had been accepted, precisely because they had offered cash!

They then had what Colin calls 'the great adventure of actually seeing the Lord supply the money'.[1]

That God wanted the fellowship to have that building was beyond doubt by now. *But it had to be prayed into being*. For the fellowship it was a time of tension and excitement. Certain people pledged to sell their houses in order to offer interest-free loans to make up the £580,000. One couple was convicted to do so by the words in Acts 4:34: '. . . those who owned lands or houses sold them, took the money and laid it at the apostles' feet.'

The only person who seemed completely calm as the months went by was Colin. He had entered the rest of faith because God had promised him the money. While praying about the project in a Singapore hotel room he had sought God's answer. 'I found myself repenting all over the place for two hours, because God never misses a trick! Perhaps it only took two hours because I wasn't even backslidden at the time.

'Suddenly I was in the throne room of God and He said to me, "I give you a million dollars" (the Singapore equivalent of the sum required). From that time on all there remained to do was thank Him.'

No one, including Colin, knew who would provide the rest of the money. But that, as Colin says, is the whole point of faith. 'If you knew where it was coming from, you wouldn't need the faith.'

So although the money came in from Singapore in a nail-biting climax a few hours before the deadline, the fellowship had to make the response of faith by thanking God for His provision: 'Believe that you have received it.' (Mark 11:24)

Sometime later Colin asked God why the money for that and other projects never came until the last moment. The reply was devastatingly logical: 'Because you don't need it till then.'

'Ask a silly question . . .' Colin thought to himself.

Francis Pym remembers acting on some practical teaching about money at The Hyde:

'We very bravely gave away ten pounds – five pounds each to two little families – and looked to God to give back the measure that we expected, because Colin had said that the measure we gave would be the measure we received. At the time we were reading a book by Oral Roberts, *A Daily Guide to Miracles*, so we expected the measure we received back to be thirty, sixty or a hundredfold.

'For about five weeks we were at the peak of our faith,

believing for a return on this ten pounds. Lo and behold, about six weeks later, I got a cheque from the tax office quite unexpectedly refunding just over three hundred pounds. We opened it in the kitchen at The Hyde and were all looking at this money and rejoicing, thinking "How marvellous! It works!" when Colin walked in. He heard what was happening and said, as only Colin can say it, "Hmm . . . Thirtyfold." That rather deflated us all.'

Living by faith was a new experience for Tim and Pam Hunt. As an insurance executive, Tim was used to going around with a wallet full of cash for business entertaining and all the other expenses of a 'comfortable' lifestyle. Once he and Pam joined the ministry, he found his wallet was empty and the company car replaced by a much older vehicle in need of tender loving care. In fact they never went without anything they needed, but the adjustment to greater dependence on God, let alone fielding criticism from their family, initially came as a shock.

'We had to learn faith for ourselves; corporate faith is one thing – believing for yourself is something else. We're better at it now because we learned to cry out to God for provision and we've seen some incredible things.'

Pam is quick to point out that prosperity was not a goal in itself:

'Colin doesn't emphasise prosperity except as a by-product of your covenant relationship with God, an incidental to the walk of faith.'

Tim, whose mother continued to regard them as 'absolutely potty', confessed that the walk of faith could be very lonely at times, but was made worthwhile by the spiritual rewards, such as the *Way of the Spirit* Bible study course they have taught together which he describes as 'unbelievable'.

After almost ten years without a pay cheque, Tim and Pam could not be persuaded that God did not want the best for them, or that He would fail to provide 'the icing on the cake. If you're faithful in the small things, the big ones seem to suddenly drop in your lap. It's exciting.'

Caroline Urquhart also discovered that God cared about her personal needs. While thanking Him for His provision for her family, she felt it would be nice to have something just for herself. Shortly afterwards she received a letter and a cheque from a woman who wanted her to use the money to buy herself a dress.

The atmosphere at The Hyde was conducive to building faith; all the equipment needed arrived after prayer. Every time something was needed, the community crowded into the kitchen to ask God for it. Grahame Scofield, the ministry's accountant, was able to record the blessing; he watched as money came in to cover all the costs, although he and his wife Elizabeth remembered all the residents bundled up in jumpers in the early days because there was no spare money for heating. As God had told Colin never to make appeals for money, it was all the more amazing when a television for the children or a computer were donated.

One of Colin's favourite expressions is 'Joy is the barometer of your faith'. All Christians should be joyful as Jesus was, 'who for the joy set before him endured the cross, scorning its shame, and sat down at the right hand of the throne of God'. (Hebrews 12:2)

Fear, doubt and unbelief are the enemies of faith: 'Everything that does not come from faith is sin.' (Romans 14:23) And clinging to old habits like doubting that God will fulfil His word, actually hinders what He wants to do in your life. 'As long as you're in negativity, you can't take a step forward,' says Colin. 'And God will leave you there. That's why some Christians go in circles, claiming, "I have these problems – I can't help it . . ." Oh yes, you can: God is ready to change your heart as soon as you ask. And of course unbelief is a sin – you should repent of your *sin* and start giving thanks in all circumstances.'

Knowing our identity in Christ is essential for a life of faith in God's word. Barbara Redmore, Colin's former secretary, recalled the effect that this truth had on new students and people at Faith Camp:

'Each year Colin would preach to them that their old selves had died, that they had new life in Christ. The old was gone and the new had come! You could just see it dawning on them as a tremendous revelation; some of them had never realised just who they were . . .'

Chapter Seven

PRAYER: THE HEARTBEAT OF REVIVAL

Sitting in the lecture room with the other Kingdom Faith students one day, listening to John McKay talking about great revivals of the past, our attention was diverted by a wailing from next door. Seeing our distraction, John stopped and listened also.

'Oh, them again,' he announced, recognising the sound, a combination of air raid sirens and Schopenhauer.

We nodded and carried on listening to John while the sirens reached a crescendo next door, interspersed with an occasional groan and followed by silence before the next crescendo began.

Even in such a spiritually intense place as Roffey, the intercession group was something else again. Consisting at that time of a research scientist, a doctor, a solicitor, two businesswomen and a language graduate, the group looked perfectly normal when not in the throes of intercession! The groans that day probably signified that they were in travail (spiritual labour); on other occasions they might be doing battle or simply 'resting in God' before scaling the next mountain. While we learned about the last great revival, they were revving up for the next one.

Historically, revival has always been preceded by prayer, by intense intercession and spiritual conflict, long before the term 'spiritual warfare' became fashionable amongst twentieth-century Christians.

Colin knows that times of revival in his ministry have been produced by prayer, by seeking God for Himself. There were two prayer meetings in his Luton church every morning and eighteen prayer groups.

Sadly, a desire to pray more, like holiness, is not near the top of everyone's 'most wanted' list. When Colin was called out of Luton, he found himself inundated with invitations to speak, especially at leaders' meetings.

'They all wanted to know the secrets of getting a sovereign move of God. So I told them that at Luton I spent at least three hours in prayer with various groups of people before midday – and I saw them switch off.'

Yonggi Cho, leader of a Korean church of 800,000, told a leaders' seminar that there were three keys to church growth: 'You pray, then you pray, and then you pray.'

Similarly five weeks of intensive prayer preceded revival at The Hyde. At that time they were not looking for revival for its own sake, however.

'People who want revival for its own sake don't get it,' says Colin. 'We *need* it, but it's a prerequisite for two things. Firstly for people to get to know God, and secondly to see the nation changed.'

After that breakthrough in 1981, there have been other times of personal revival for many members of the ministry. Some found they would be woken by God at night to pray. Colin himself still has many broken nights, but knows that the small hours are sometimes the only opportunity for him to spend uninterrupted time with the Lord.

'When the spirit of prayer is on you, you can't do anything else. You often get to places with the Lord when sacrifice is involved, when He's wanting us to move ahead with Him. Then *everything* must take second place, including ministry.'

Happily Colin and others who intercede at length have discovered the truth of the words, 'Those who hope in the Lord will renew their strength.' (Isaiah 40:31)

A spirit of prayer is a sign of personal revival. We do not need to wait for it to descend, however; once we start praying earnestly, the spirit of prayer comes! When Charles Finney taught that we can have revival whenever we want it, he meant that an individual or group of believers can revive their faith by leaving behind all that is ungodly and pressing forward to seek God.

Colin teaches that two things always accompany what

God does in revival: 'God's people become concerned with personal holiness because they're drawing near to a holy God. And then God's people *cry out* to God for the lost. It's not saying polite prayers, but feeling lost yourself.'

A burning concern for the lost came as a new experience for many of the Kingdom Faith team who may have prayed for certain relatives and friends to be saved but had not felt God's concern for the other millions. Yet after times of seeking the Lord as a body, many of them changed. Spiritual priorities were shifted as they recognised that everyone is called to be an intercessor.

Team member David Hazeldine, who believes God has promised revival will be 'soon', has experienced this change: 'There's an intensity, the desire for revival. I'm just living, eating, breathing revival. In Revelation the Spirit and the bride say, "Come" to the Lord Jesus. That's my prayer. A couple of days ago, I said, "We're so hungry for You, Lord." And He replied, "It's not the fact that you're hungry, because I would be there if you were hungry. It's the fact that you need Me."

'In revival many people become Christians because they realise their need of God. In the charismatic renewal there was repentance, but it didn't extend to conveying the fear of the Lord to the nation. It didn't affect the Christians enough to affect the non-Christians. A revelation of hell changed my prayer for the lost, too. When you continually walk in repentance and let the Holy Spirit do what He wants to do, He changes your life.'

Amongst the others who discovered that prayer is the key to revival was Colin's secretary Helena Croft. She was with Colin when he went through his 'Gethsemane' and after that crucial time found herself enveloped in a spirit of prayer.

'Prayer is hard work; you've got to keep going and keep praying, but the more you do it, the more you want to do it. The struggle, the battle, the breaking through, are all part of it because we are in a battle.'

Her husband Jonathan agrees. 'The place where you need to pray is in the holy of holies – that's where you get your answers. If you're there, it means your heart is pure and holy, so you'll only be praying "Thy Kingdom come, Thy will be done as it is in heaven", which includes preventing and permitting things to happen.'

Our call to pray

It is, however, always tempting to wonder why, since God is God, He needs our prayers. Surely He doesn't need us to activate the revival He has already planned since the beginning of the world?

'Part of the key is the fact that He has given us free will,' explains Elizabeth Allan, who leads the Kingdom Faith intercession group. Her specific call is to pray for revival, which, she believes, is the reason she has been led to Kingdom Faith, whose vision is totally for revival. After giving up a demanding career as a research scientist for an even more demanding call, she has no doubt about the necessity of God's people praying.

'He tells us to pray, "Thy will be done", so He wants our will to come into alignment with His. Prayer is a way of changing us, so that our will becomes one with His so we then *desire* His will.

'By praying, we invite God into a situation, so He is then free to act. He doesn't force His way into a situation, so He will not force revival onto people who are not ready for it; He wants us to come into unity with His perfect plans and purposes and then to pray them into being, in accordance with Jesus' promise: "If you abide (remain) in me and my words abide in you, ask whatever you wish, and it shall be given to you. This is to my Father's glory . . ."' (John 15:7)

She points out that Jesus' famous words, 'Here I am! I stand at the door and knock. If anyone hears my voice and opens the door, I will come in and eat with him, and he with me' (Revelation 3:20) are aimed at believers: 'Jesus could easily open the door Himself and come in, but He stands outside waiting for us to invite Him in.'

Colin confirms that when God calls us to prayer, it is not to initiate something but to become part of heavenly activity: 'Jesus never has a day off – He's not on shift work. He's always reigning, always interceding for us. That's why the Holy Spirit is urging us to pray all the time (He says "Pray without ceasing") and why in real worship you lose track of time because you're so aware of God's presence.'

He stresses again the importance of knowing God's will for our prayers: 'Get God's mind on something so you can join in His intercession and be sensitive to what the Holy Spirit wants to pray in and through and for us. You can even ask Him what He's interceding for you personally.'

Praying with faith and authority

Too many 'mature' Christians have been persuaded by their experience that God's promises are somehow not for them. Yet failure to take Jesus at His word means that these Christians are in the same place of unbelief as non-Christians. They need to enter – by faith – into that dimension of believing God, which is their inheritance.

Praying in faith came naturally to Elizabeth Allan because it sprang from her close relationship with God. When she was converted in a Damascus Road type of experience, she received a powerful revelation of God's love which many Christians do not receive for years. Her new-found, intense awareness of God's love and faithfulness prevented any doubt that God would answer prayer.

'There is rest and joy in true faith,' Elizabeth has discovered. 'There is no striving involved.'

Standing on God's word (Ephesians 6:13–14) means lifting up the situation to Him and thanking Him while you rest in the knowledge that He will do what He has said He will do.

'You know when you believe and you know when you half believe and you're trying to convince God, yourself and everybody else that you believe, and you know when you don't believe at all,' says Colin.

'Faith is not going around saying, "I believe, I believe, O Lord, I believe!" It is simply knowing that God will do what He has promised.'

Dan Chesney believes that the words in Philippians 4:6 explain why many Christians fail in prayer:

'Do not be anxious about anything, but in *everything*, by prayer and petition, with thanksgiving, present your requests to God.'(italics mine)

Ten minutes of 'dreamy' prayer each morning is not enough. 'The enemy will carry on struggling against you all day,' explains Dan. 'Rulers oppose you and every area of your Christian life all day and every day. They don't give up. You see miracles in Africa because they understand spiritual warfare, that it's demons behind sickness and trouble. So we must wrestle in prayer. Satan tries to encourage us to pray *for* people and not *against* the demons causing trouble. You can pray for someone to be saved, but not be praying against the god of this world who has blinded them.'

One of the privileges God has granted His children is authority over all the powers of the enemy:

> 'I have given you authority to trample on snakes and scorpions and to overcome all the power of the enemy; nothing will harm you. However, do not rejoice that the spirits submit to you, but rejoice that your names are written in heaven.' (Luke 10:19–20)

Once believers know they have authority, not through being a 'better' Christian but simply through the shed blood of Jesus, they are dangerous to the devil. The existence of angels and demons is thoroughly scriptural. Less, perhaps, is known of their activities, but interesting revelations have been received by Colin and Dan. For example, when bookings for conferences and the annual Faith Camp fell suddenly in 1992, Colin went before God. The Lord told him, 'The reason that bookings are lower is that the enemy has mustered his forces against the conferences because of what I am doing here.'

The implication of this revelation is clearly that the forces of evil can influence people's minds to persuade them against taking certain steps. People may be discouraged by thoughts and circumstances which may not necessarily even appear to be negative. It is easy to think, 'Why go to another Christian meeting when I have so many other involvements?' Or 'There's a recession on.

Are you wise to commit yourself to a holiday at this stage?' And such thoughts are often perfectly valid; it is up to the individual to take the time to pray and seek the Lord about each decision.

In the case of the camp bookings, all the Kingdom Faith team and students prayed for about ten minutes one lunchtime, followed, no doubt, by much private prayer. Two weeks later the bookings, which had lagged several hundred behind the previous year's numbers at the same time, exceeded the previous year's total by one hundred and fifty. Visitors were still turning up once the camp had started, bringing that year's attendance to a record level.

Similarly when Dan's house was burgled, he asked God the reason. His had been the only house in his road with no alarm and yet no break-ins for the last three years. Why had it suddenly been burgled? God's answer surprised him: 'Your angels were unable to stop them breaking in because you stopped praying.'

These are just examples of the believer's authority over the powers of the enemy, an authority which is impressive when its results are seen.

In Luton, Colin experienced cases of sick people being referred by doctors and psychiatrists to be prayed for by the church.

'The world isn't interested in words like "authority" and "in the name of Jesus", but in results,' claims Colin. 'This is what Jesus expects of our prayer lives. Results won't be yours because you prayed, but because you *believed* when you prayed. I can recite many cases of having spoken to situations and receiving what I prayed for, but what concerns me are cases where I didn't receive because I didn't believe – I had doubt in my heart. And God gives you what you believe in your heart.

'God isn't a fool. If you spend a good part of the day speaking out things that contradict what God desires, you can't expect your prayers to suddenly get results.'

He believes that the famous verses about 'binding and loosing' and coming together in Jesus' name are some of the most misused verses in the Bible:

'I tell you the truth, whatever you bind on earth will

be bound in heaven, and whatever you loose on earth will be loosed in heaven.' (Matthew 18:18)

Colin explains that 'on earth' can include the spiritual realms, because they affect what is happening on earth. Nor does the passage mention demons; although we have authority to bind demons, we also have authority to bind or prevent *any* ungodly situations on earth, and to loose or permit *any* things which are in God's heavenly will.

> 'Again, I tell you that if two of you on earth agree about anything you ask for, it will be done for you by my Father in heaven. For where two or three come together in my name, there am I with them.' (Matthew 18:19–20)

These verses have also been misunderstood, with the result that 'in Jesus' name' is automatically tacked onto the end of prayers that might be lacking in real faith.

'Coming together in the name of Jesus does not mean turning up at a prayer meeting or service, but coming together *in faith*,' says Colin.

Praying through to victory

Both spiritual warfare and intercession are expected of Christians. Paul spoke of 'wrestling in prayer' (Colossians 4:12) which no more speaks of nice quiet prayers than the groans which can come forth when the Holy Spirit is allowed to intercede through us:

> '. . . the Spirit helps us in our weakness. We do not know what we ought to pray for, but the Spirit himself intercedes for us with groans that words cannot express. And he who searches our hearts knows the mind of the Spirit, because the Spirit intercedes for the saints in accordance with God's will.' (Romans 8:26–27)

Prayer of this sort is not for a spiritual elite; we are all intercessors.

'The grief and compassion and anguish that is felt in true travail is from the heart of God. It is His heart being expressed in and through us in intercession. It is neither emotionalism nor crying in unbelief – which would be fruitless. But as we pray through the burden that God puts on our heart, we will reach that place of breakthrough in the spirit, a place of joy, peace and victory with the assurance that God will answer,' explains Elizabeth Allan.

Such 'travail' is common in intercession. Colin teaches believers that they have the right to rule, reign, govern and dominate the spiritual atmosphere in the name of the Lord Jesus. To see victory in a situation, however, it is often necessary to 'pray through' until victory is sensed.

Each Wednesday morning the whole Kingdom Faith ministry team comes together to intercede for God's revival work. Like the intercession team, they have been taught by Colin to 'pray through' to a place of victory in the spiritual realms:

> 'For our struggle is not against flesh and blood, but against the rulers, against the authorities, against the powers of this dark world and against the spiritual forces of evil in the heavenly realms.' (Ephesians 6:12)

Since the Kingdom Faith Church is expecting to reach people in a twenty-five mile radius, the whole area is frequently prayed for, sometimes using a map of towns, and often praying for those in authority such as those in local government as well as local Members of Parliament. This is a typical example of the need to 'wrestle' in prayer.

'Just claiming the area for God isn't enough,' says Dan Chesney. 'You've got to keep going until you know you've got a breakthrough in those specific circumstances – then you can pray the prayer of faith, agreeing together that God's will for that place or people shall be done.' It is always important to set the objective. In a healing situation the leader might say 'We're going to pray through until the cancer is clear' rather than simply, 'We'll pray for Jack.'

Any unbelief must be cleared out by ensuring everyone present believes in the objective. Jesus cleared out all the unbelievers from the room when He prayed for Jairus' daughter who was raised from the dead. Unbelief opposes faith.

Colin will challenge the people praying as to whether or not they are committed to getting the right answer – not just any answer. He quotes the parable of the widow pleading with the judge: 'God isn't deaf, but our prayers have to defeat the powers of darkness first.'

With the objective set, everyone starts to pray in tongues. Each group praying must have a leader who is sensitive enough to know when the objective is accomplished. Colin warns them to beware of 'cheap' victories:

'You can come to a place of peace, but that's not victory. It's a resting place, a plateau, but then you must continue up the mountain. The battle belongs to the Lord and He's praying in and through us and speaking to us by His Holy Spirit who will show us specific areas to clear out by praying against them. We win three-nil every time but we still have to play the match first!'

Praying for the nation

Listening to the tape accompanying Colin's book *My Dear Son* changed Elizabeth Allan's perspective on praying for the nation. At the end of the tape, Colin, speaking what he believes is directly from the Lord asks, 'Do you believe I will change the spiritual as well as the political, social and moral climate of the nation?'

Until then Elizabeth had indeed believed He would revive the Church and bring a spiritual awakening, with the Church being cleansed and multitudes coming into the Kingdom of God. She also believed He would morally change those in revival and those converted in the awakening, as well as changing the government and bringing godly leaders to political power.

Yet she realised she did not have the vision or faith for a massive political, social and moral change in the nation.

'The Lord showed me that if I didn't have that faith, I would set my sights too low in prayer. There would be whole vast areas where the Lord wanted to work that I wouldn't be reaching in prayer. And if I did pray into those areas, I wouldn't have the necessary faith for the prayers to be effective.'

The Holy Spirit confirmed this by reminding her of the importance of resolute prayers:

> 'But when he asks, he must believe and not doubt, because he who doubts is like a wave of the sea, blown and tossed by the wind. That man should not think he will receive anything from the Lord; he is a double-minded man, unstable in all he does. (James 1:6–7)

These lines helped inspire her to pray for vision and faith.

'I asked that He would start me praying for the nation to be changed not only spiritually, but politically, socially and morally on a large scale. Obviously we can believe that God will work in specific situations, for individuals or whole groups of people God puts on our hearts to pray for, like drug addicts or satanists, but changing the nation politically, socially and morally *en masse* requires a different level of faith altogether. There is a vast difference between praying in hope and praying in faith. God wants to take us to a whole new dimension of praying in faith for the nation.'

Several weeks later this concept was confirmed for Elizabeth at the annual Faith Camp by guest speaker Ray McCauley. His Rhema Church in South Africa has been used by God to have an impact on the nation's spiritual, political, social and moral life. The demise of the apartheid system owes much to the prayer and example of this and other churches. In their sixteen-thousand-strong church, black and white have always worshipped side by side. Now, with six hundred new churches planted and a new one being planted every two days, these churches have helped the total number of active Christians in South Africa reach 20 per cent of the population. Ray McCauley is known nationwide and has played an active part in peace negotiations. A multi-racial school founded by his church has survived despite powerful opposition and persecution. The ways in which Christians are influencing the fabric of that society gave Elizabeth fresh faith for Britain.

'As a result of hearing God and learning about a living example of a nation being changed, I've emerged with far greater faith for Britain. Now my praying for the nation has changed. I'm far bolder in praying for areas where I previously had little vision, and I'm really expecting God to work in those areas.

'Years ago, shortly before I came to Kingdom Faith, the Lord spoke to me about sowing and reaping. He said, "You reap as you sow. If you sow in ones and twos, you will reap in ones and twos. If you sow into the lives of millions, you will reap in the lives of millions." He explained to me that yes, it's good to pray for individuals and small groups of people, but if that's all I do then it's only those lives that are having prayer sown into them, so the reaping will only be in small numbers. But if we sow into the lives of millions in prayer, then the reaping will be in millions. So at the same time as speaking to me about having faith that He would change the nation, He was also reminding me about sowing in prayer into the lives of millions in the nation.'

The cost of intercession

People often think that prayer is an easy get-out, the stay-at-home option; but true, fervent intercession can be very costly physically, spiritually, mentally and emotionally, maintains Elizabeth.

'We need to be willing to pray all night when the Lord asks us. We have to be prepared to share in His grief over the state of the Church and the lost in the nation. A bland "If it be Thy will, Lord, send revival" is a waste of time. It needs to be a cry from the heart, with sacrificial giving in prayer, being prepared to be part of the answer to our own prayers wherever He directs. As we pray, God so works in our hearts and in the situation, that we discern His voice and will act according to the leading of His Spirit instead of trying to work things out in our own strength.'

Elizabeth has experienced being 'part of the answer' when she was accepted for weekly visits to the psychiatric and drug addict wards of Holloway Prison where she can talk freely about Jesus to women with broken lives. (Also explained in Chapter Two.) With Joy Pedder, a former Kingdom Faith student and church member, she is starting to see amazing conversions take place and is praising God for letting her go to prison!

One instance where she knew the cost of intercession but was not called to be part of the answer occurred during the 1991 Gulf War. Praying for much of each night ensured she had little sleep during the hostilities. Before and after office hours she was also praying about the war's outcome, with Harry and Jane Creswell. Harry, an ex-major who administers Kingdom Faith Church and organises the annual Faith Camp with military precision, is always keen on routing God's enemies through tactical intercession.

After the air bombardment the Allied troops were due to liberate Kuwait City, approaching it by land from Saudi Arabia. The Lord told them to pray that the Iraqi occupiers would evacuate the city before the Allies arrived in order to avoid protracted and bloody street fighting. On the morning of the third day of the ground-war, God told Elizabeth to pray specifically that the city would be liberated that day. All day she prayed obediently, yet even by midnight the television and radio gave no indication that the Allies were more than a few miles over the border; they were expected to take a long time negotiating obstructions between the border and the city. Yet she had total peace in her spirit that God had done it. Here was a case where it was vital to hold on to God's specific word in the face of contradictory circumstances.

Not until 3.20 pm the next day was it announced that Kuwait City had been liberated the previous evening after the Iraqis had fled.

Praying in the Spirit

Praying in tongues is often the most effective way of discerning and praying in accordance with God's will.

'I often find that when I pray in tongues, God changes my perspective on a situation,' says Elizabeth. 'I may end up praying something in English which is completely different from my original idea of how to pray before I prayed in tongues.'

Elizabeth believes that even those baptised in the Holy Spirit can miss out on the full benefits of praying in tongues. They may be deceived into thinking that it is rather meaningless and less fruitful than praying in English. But when we pray in tongues we know we are praying in the will of God since the gift is of the Holy Spirit and therefore should not be underestimated. St Paul says: 'I will pray with my spirit, but I will also pray with my mind.' (1 Corinthians 14:15)

John McKay points out that in the context of 1 Corinthians 14:13–15 this means 'I will pray in tongues and also pray the interpretation in English'. In this way both our minds and spirit are praying in the perfect will of God.

Elizabeth also believes that at times it is not appropriate for us to know what we are praying for in tongues. St Paul says, 'He who prays in a tongue utters mysteries with his spirit.' (1 Corinthians 14:2) This may be to protect someone or because what we are praying is simply too deep for words. It may be because our own ideas of how to pray in that area are too entrenched for us to be fully open to the Holy Spirit's interpretation. However, as we continue to pray in tongues, we gain God's perspective.

This can be extremely valuable when praying about a pastoral situation where one does not wish to share personal or 'incriminating' details. Thus a prayer group can be asked to intercede in the Spirit for a situation without knowing who or what they are praying about. Rather than group members struggling to articulate prayers in English about a situation whose direness has been merely hinted at, they are completely free to hear from the Holy Spirit. 'One then hears from God with remarkable clarity,' claims Elizabeth. 'The Holy Spirit gives scriptures, words of knowledge and prophetic insights which prove to be keys to a breakthrough in the situation.'

An amusing incident during her early days in the Kingdom Faith team showed why obedience to the Holy Spirit's prompting is more important than precise interpretation of tongues. She knew that part of her call was to pray for Colin's role in revival, but she was surprised when she found herself praying in tongues at some point during the praise and worship at almost every meeting. She had no peace if she stopped praying and returned to worshipping God with the rest. Five minutes later, invariably, Colin would stand up to speak. After asking God what she was praying for, He told her to open her eyes the next time it happened.

'I noticed that Colin was opening his Bible and beginning to read. The next day the same happened again and I found that every prompting to pray in tongues coincided with Colin opening his Bible in preparation for his sermon. The Lord has shown me since then that when He simply starts me praying in tongues at other times of the day, it is often for Colin while he is reading the Bible.'

One of the gifts of the Spirit is speaking in 'different kinds of tongues'. (1 Corinthians 12:10) This indicates that any individual may have several prayer languages. For example, one day Elizabeth found herself using a new tongue while praying with her intercession group for Colin. As usual they had asked God for His prayer agenda at the start of their meeting. He indicated that they should pray for Colin for the years of 1994–1999. While doing so, Elizabeth found herself praying in a new language.

Receiving life

God also wants us to receive from Him. A successful method used by Colin's church in Luton resulted in many healings and conversions from the eighteen groups involved. They used no words of their own, only the words of Scripture, because as Jesus said, 'The words I have spoken to you are spirit and they are life'. (John 6:63) They became the most powerful groups for healing that Colin has ever known.

It is helpful to be led through the first meditation to

accustom oneself to its simple discipline of confessing sins, casting one's burdens onto the Lord and forgiving others. The idea is to spend a very short time doing this in order to be prepared to receive from God. 'Thirty seconds should be plenty to cast all your burdens on the Lord,' says Colin, 'and a minute if you're in a real bad state.'

Then, rather than using their own words to pray 'Will you please heal John', a group would take a specific scripture of healing or peace, such as 'I am the Lord who heals you, John' thus personalising it by adding the individual's name. For the first five minutes they would receive the words for themselves – and in this way they received the power of the Holy Spirit and were able to impart it to others. On each occasion they prayed for just six to eight people with whom they had personal contact. 'The idea was to get people on and off the list as soon as possible,' Colin explained. 'By believing the words they prayed for those people, they were fulfilling the commission not to pray for but to heal the sick. It taught me the great principle that life is in the word of God itself. If you're receiving positive truth regularly, there's no room for the negative.'

Significantly, members of these groups very rarely became sick themselves.

It was partly the success of this method of prayer which proved to Colin that hurting people needed the word of God, not pseudo-psychological counselling methods. His church was happily receiving direct from God through His word, in the days before counselling and inner healing became popular.

Later Colin turned these meditations into a book, *Listen and Live*, which is popular amongst members of the ministry. Even today, if Colin is feeling over-burdened, he will go into his study and repeat to himself the words, 'My peace I give to you, Colin'.

He also recommends praying for children using this method. Parents should receive for themselves first, then hold their hand over the child and say, 'I am the Lord who heals you, child.'

One group in Luton concentrated on praying for non-believing family members with astonishing results. 'Three teenage daughters came to the Lord within three to four weeks and all went on to fruitful Christian ministry.'

Using this method also had a remarkable effect on worship. 'There would be sudden silences in the midst of high praise when everyone went into receiving mode – five to ten minutes is a very long time in public worship.'

At the time it was further proof that God was doing something special in that church. Colin taught the method to all new church members in their 'Know Jesus' groups.

'I didn't have the remotest idea why we were doing many of these things – we just did what God told us. It was God who was instilling these things in us.'

There is tremendous variety in prayer when the Holy Spirit is allowed His way. What led to Dan Chesney's time of revival was a three-month period in America when he was gripped by a spirit of prayer. 'Sometimes I was on the floor groaning about the condition of California; sometimes it was loud, aggressive tongues; sometimes I was confessing the word while pacing the floor; sometimes I was weeping in brokenness when the Holy Spirit moved upon me and I saw my sin and waywardness; sometimes I simply experienced great joy.'

Prayer: the key to personal revival

Four key things brought Elizabeth Allan into personal revival, completely changing her life, over a ten-day period in January 1992. Three out of the four keys were connected with prayer. The first occurred after Colin gave an address about 'resting in God'. This is deeper, he explained, than 'putting your feet up and having nice woosey feelings'.

According to Elizabeth, it is entering into the holy of holies and loving God with all our heart, mind, soul and strength, and letting Him love us.

'It is deep, intimate communion with Him, too deep for words, where we worship Him in spirit and in truth. There is nothing hindering our communion with Him and we know we are at peace with Him. As we rest in God, we become one with Him.'

Although Elizabeth loved resting in God, there was

always 'a nagging suspicion' in the back of her mind that she really ought to be doing something active and more obviously useful.

What changed her perspective on resting in God was when Colin shared a revelation that God had given him. Colin had found that when he was able to rest in God after engaging in powerful spiritual warfare and intercession before a meeting, the power of God released in the meeting was greater. This bore out the truth that if we abide in Jesus and He abides in us, we will bear much fruit. (John 15:5) When we rest in God, we step out of the way and let the Holy Spirit in us speak and act. According to Colin, the Lord said to him, 'I don't want *you* to minister. I crucified you; that's what I think of you. *I* want to speak and minister *through* you.'

Colin realised that by resting in God, he was getting out of God's way and giving the Holy Spirit the freedom to minister.

That revelation freed Elizabeth to rest in God at any time. The new freedom made a dramatic difference to her life:

'It brought me into a more constant communion with God and there was a very deep, abiding sense of His presence at all times. For three weeks I felt as if I was in heaven. It was like a foretaste of revival. God's presence was so strong and I had such an amazing depth of love for everyone.'

The second key happened a couple of days later when God gave her a deeper revelation of the Holy Spirit in her. Again, it was directly as a result of a talk by Colin. 'I realised afresh that I have been crucified with Christ, and it is indeed no longer I who live, but Christ who lives in me. All I had to do was get out of the way of the Holy Spirit in me and let Him do the speaking and acting. I realised that I didn't need years and years of discipleship or a closer walk with God to be used by God. All I had to do was reckon myself dead and let the Holy Spirit in me do and say whatever He wanted. If He asked me to do something, however difficult or impossible it might seem, it was possible because He in me would do it.'

The third key came about four days later when, out

of the blue, the Lord said to her one night, 'My word says "pray without ceasing". That means you can do it twenty-four hours a day, both awake and asleep. At the moment you're praying without ceasing when you're awake, but you're not praying when you're asleep. I wouldn't ask you to do anything that you couldn't do – certainly apart from me you can do nothing – but you can do all things through Christ who strengthens you. My Holy Spirit is an intercessor and He lives in you, so ask My Holy Spirit in you to be constantly praying as you sleep. You also have a spirit – you're not just body, soul and Holy Spirit. St Paul said, "I will pray with my spirit; but I will also pray with my mind", so ask the Holy Spirit to also keep your spirit and your mind constantly interceding as you sleep.'

Elizabeth realised that praying without ceasing was a command, not just a good idea or an unattainable ideal. Nor was it something she needed to strive to achieve, because God would provide the means, showing her that she was supposed to pray in her sleep – there was obviously no way she could keep herself praying in her sleep. 'This was a beautiful demonstration of God providing the enabling to carry out His commands.'

That night she went to bed excited. All the time previously wasted sleeping would now be used to pray directly in accordance with God's will as directed by the Holy Spirit. When she woke up the next morning she was transformed. 'The least thing God had done overnight was to heal my stammer, which I'd developed as a child, and had for twenty-six years. He had made many other deep changes overnight, too.'

After that her life began to move forwards rapidly, as she found herself stretched in every direction, doing things she would never have dreamed of before. As well as extra prayer, she was able to speak to interested groups about intercession.

'I know it's the added hours of prayer in my sleep that are largely enabling me to go into this new dimension of spiritual activity,' she claims.

Elizabeth feels that every believer would benefit enormously from taking seriously this particular command from God. 'Praying without ceasing is not an option – it's both a command and invitation.'

Four days later, the fourth key emerged. Colin spoke to the team and new students about pulling down strongholds in their minds – wrong thinking and attitudes. (2 Corinthians 10:4–5) In the short time following, he encouraged them to ask the Holy Spirit to pinpoint these hindrances to holiness. The Lord told Elizabeth that there were strongholds of fear in her life; specifically fear in relating to people. She repented and made the verbal command, 'In the name of Jesus I pull down that stronghold of fear of man.' Thus she was set free from her fears.

Everything that happened in that ten-day period served to change her radically and equip her for new areas of work, including addressing groups of people on prayer (previously impossible with her stammer) and working with 'hard cases' in Holloway Prison.

Before Elizabeth tries any new ventures she shuts herself away with God for thorough preparation in prayer, aware that, as Colin says, 'A Christian is only as good as his prayer life, a fact that's too true to be comfortable.'

He also emphasises listening to God, and found that his book *My Dear Child* revolutionised many people's prayer lives because they learned to listen to the words of assurance which build faith: 'Babbling displays an absence of faith. Why does Jesus tell you to shut yourself away? Because that's where He gives His love. Meetings and church can never replace the secret place where you meet your Father. Praying with others is no substitute for Father and me. Jesus is saying, "You'll miss it if all you do is babble, pouring out your needs. I know your needs before you speak them – be still and know that I AM God."'

A life of intercession

The importance of listening to and receiving refreshment from God was realised many years ago by Elizabeth Scofield, who found herself called to intercession in general and in particular for Colin. She and Elizabeth

Allan still meet weekly to pray for him. Before encountering Colin at East Molesey (his temporary home before The Hyde), she and her husband Grahame were at Holy Trinity Church, Hounslow, already using the gifts of the Holy Spirit and working as part of their prayer team. The idea of seeing results for prayer was 'kicked out of me long ago', she says. She became used to praying for people whom she might never see again.

'In a sense we are only the Lord's channels for prayer – or intercession. It's really all up to Him. He registers every single prayer in heaven and you just praise God that He's heard, He's there and you are somehow co-operating with the Spirit. I feel the call to pray, which is on all our lives, is so special, because it draws us so close to our Father's heart. You couldn't be closer in any work for Him than in intercession, in laying hands on people or praying on your own.'

Elizabeth's introduction to Christianity came from a devout nanny, 'a beautiful Christian', who impressed Elizabeth by her close relationship with Jesus and her confident exercise of spiritual authority. When Nanny thundered, 'Get thee behind me, Satan', the young Elizabeth would think, 'Ooh, I bet he jolly well does.'

From bathtime choruses and bedtime prayers she grew up talking naturally to Jesus herself, believing that when someone was sick you should pray for them and they should get healed. 'No one told me that, but I had a definite feeling this was what should happen.' Wartime was spent in a 'high' church which had a strong sense of community engendered by the vicar. 'He encouraged everyone to look after each other, and of course *everyone* was praying then.'

In her late thirties she was born again and was grateful to God for baptising her with His Holy Spirit, because the gift of tongues not only allowed her to pray fluently in an unknown language but released her to pray more confidently in English.

She has discovered that prayer is listening first and then speaking. 'It's as important to hear God beforehand as it is to give Him the prayer.' So if God has laid on her heart a subject for prayer, she needs to hear how to pray about it. To this end she believes she is not meant to get too involved in 'the razzmatazz of life'.

She uses silences a lot in prayer. In those moments she is guided as to whom or what to pray for. 'I don't always get it right, but I know God is gracious and forgives me. When I confess I haven't got it right, He picks me up and dusts me down and puts me back on course. The prompting of the Spirit is important, but I think it is *very* important to listen in prayer.'

Elizabeth has learned the secret of letting the Holy Spirit govern her prayer time. She believes everyone is called to pray in their own ways as the Holy Spirit leads them. This way it does not become a chore.

'I think, quite honestly, I'd cease to pray if somebody gave me a ritual for prayer, or certain steps I'd have to follow. And I do use Colin's *Listen and Live* during the day because I personally find that one of the best books for me.'

Now her children are grown up Elizabeth is able to devote much of the day to prayer. She is grateful that her time with God is fairly structured:

'It must be the Lord who keeps me to it, because I'm not a structured person. Obviously I might have to do other things in-between, but the flow of prayer is fairly continuous. It sounds rigid, but it's not, because the content of that time will change.'

Her mornings have fallen into a certain routine.

'Each morning I try to praise God immediately my mind is actually conscious, and I have a time of simply focussing on Him and worshipping Him. Then, having "the full armour of God" (Ephesians 6:10–18), I take the authority of Jesus over our household, our family, our work and whoever we're involved with during the day. That's purely in English.'

A time of listening follows. Writing down what God says was something Colin taught the Bethany Fellowship, to which Elizabeth and her husband Grahame belonged from its inception. Colin still begins his day in this way; over the years he has amassed many notebooks of revelations from God.

Next, Elizabeth uses a devotional reading plan and still

gets excited at the frequency with which it incorporates what God has already told her. Breakfast and Bible reading follow, Grahame having had his breakfast and scripture reading separately.

Her time of prayer is not completely isolated from her husband's time with the Lord, however. As well as sharing scriptures which seem relevant to their circumstances or those for whom they have prayed, they pray together last thing at night after watching the television news. 'It's not that we don't talk to one another in the mornings, but we give each other that space to hear from God.'

After breakfast Elizabeth concentrates on bringing needs before God, but first she gets right with Him, asking for a pure heart and confessing 'anything that's been there that hasn't been pleasing to the Lord'.

She asks Jesus to come into her life afresh, 'to walk, talk and pray with me', and invites the Holy Spirit to fill her, their family and fellowship and those who work with them. She tells the Holy Spirit, 'This is Your day, and as I walk in it may I hear what You're saying.' Then she expects that to happen: 'Even if it's a disastrous day, I know it was given to God.'

She prays for those dear to her next, for her family, aware that sometimes there is nobody else to pray for them. 'That's a very special time.'

Having done what she calls the more formal way of praying, she goes off with a cup of tea to read the newspapers and hear what God is saying through them; after that she goes into 'free prayer', able to target her prayers as God leads. Like Elizabeth Allan, she was praying through the 1991 Gulf War. 'Millions of us were called to stand in the gap at that time. Every time it looked as if missiles were going to hit Israel, I was really rebuking them!'

After the Allies' victory, she was surprised at how exhausted she felt, and much of her praying time over the next couple of months was spent simply receiving God's peace.

As a Christian she can never be fatalistic about world events; when a newscaster announces that some catastrophe looks inevitable she cries out inwardly to God.

'I really go for it in my spirit. I cry to God that it mustn't happen, there *is* hope even when reporters say there isn't, but He must bring that hope.'

Anyone looking at the needs of those around them and of the nation could easily feel daunted, floundering in a sea of spoken and unspoken prayer requests. But Elizabeth stresses that each of us is only asked to pray for certain things. 'I know I could go to India and be dying inside all day long, but I haven't been called to do that. And someone can come up and ask me to pray about something and I can pray quite well, but the actual anointing only comes when the Holy Spirit gives that push.'

Dan Chesney confirms what Elizabeth has discovered; each of us has a 'prayer assignment', a special responsibility to pray for specific areas or people.

'It's up to us to fulfil our assignment and not to leave it to others; I can't pray other people's assignments as well as all my own!'

Elizabeth Scofield is one of many Christians around the country who has been praying over many years for God's will to be done in particular areas of British life. As we pray, we too must each ask God to reveal our own special part in His plans to bring revival to Britain.

Chapter Eight

THE COST OF WORSHIP

'My heart is steadfast, O God, my heart is steadfast;
I will sing and make music.
Awake, my soul! Awake, harp and lyre! I will awaken the dawn.' (Psalm 57:7–8)

'Praising God can seriously damage your problems,' says Carol Owen, one of Kingdom Faith's worship leaders. And she should know. Almost daily, she and others have to lead around a hundred people into the presence of the living God.

Singing and making music to God is thoroughly scriptural, yet in practice it varies enormously from one church and one tradition to another. No leader in the charismatic movement will deny its importance in concentrating people's minds, hearts and spirits on God. Most would argue that it is only by putting aside worldly concerns that Christians can return in their spirits to where they belong, to the throne room of God.

Even at a Bible College like Kingdom Faith, not everyone is obviously rejoicing to come into the house of the Lord at 8.30 a.m. although the students' timetable tells them to start waiting on the Lord at 6.30 a.m.

And while main Kingdom Faith meetings are now preceded by an hour's open prayer meeting, visitors unable to arrive before the main meeting must be helped to come into God's presence. All this has to be overcome. Hence the vital role of the anointed worship leader, sensitive to the Holy Spirit's leading.

One particularly beautiful example of using the right

music for the right moment happens at Kingdom Faith baptismal services. As the baptised person emerges from the water, a song is played which usually sums up the testimony they gave beforehand, such as *I have been crucified with Christ*, *Celebrate the goodness of the Lord* or *I am a new creation*. The significance of the song on that occasion will probably remain with the baptised person all their lives.

Preachers rely on the effectiveness of a good music ministry to set the spiritual scene before they speak to a meeting. When both are listening to the Holy Spirit, the worship leader will frequently select songs which fit the theme of the message before it has been given.

Colin Urquhart has seen the need for ministry to individuals at meetings diminish to the point that a prayer line is rarely seen. As part of the move towards encouraging believers to develop faith for themselves and others, people at Kingdom Faith meetings are often asked to pray with the people around them. After the main address Colin, Dan Chesney or another speaker may give words of knowledge to their listeners, telling them that God is healing certain diseases, or they may ask everyone to stand to pray about an area of their lives of particular concern to God.

The ideal, however, is for everyone to have such a vibrant relationship with God that they receive the assurance that all their needs have been met by Jesus on the cross as they worship Him. 'True worship,' says Colin, 'should simply be the overflow of a loving heart towards God, unaffected by circumstances.'

The apostle Paul wrote from prison that we should rejoice in all circumstances, which is difficult to obey when we feel as if we're bound in a prison of the emotions. Yet Colin often preaches that God will move in our circumstances as soon as we begin to praise Him for who He is.

'Of course,' he says, 'you could go for counselling instead, but that's longer, less effective and results in you tiring out someone else as well.'

He is not insensitive to those who really have cause to mourn, but knows it is not God's purpose for us to be in mourning permanently, because Christians should be aware they are living under the New Covenant. In the year of the Lord's favour proclaimed by Isaiah, God has sent Jesus to 'comfort all who mourn'. Thus anyone who has the Holy Spirit has the 'oil of gladness instead of mourning, and a garment of praise instead of a spirit of despair.' (Isaiah 61:3)

The 'garment of praise' should be visible:

'It's not an undervest of praise to be worn under a cloak of despair! When you don't rejoice because you don't feel like it, you play into the devil's hands.'

Confronted with an assembly of people of whom perhaps 50 per cent are determined to praise God, the burden on musicians is considerable. They in turn have to seek God for His strength to fulfil His purposes for that meeting rather than to simply perform music to the best of their ability.

Music at Kingdom Faith sounds modern and is vigorously performed on the piano, keyboard, guitars (traditional and electric) and drums. Judging from the sizes of the meetings, most visitors love the exuberance and pace of the tunes and lyrics. The songs are mainly written by the resident worship leaders.

Carol and Colin Owen, the main worship leaders at Roffey Place, found that God changed the focus of their songwriting:

'We came from a church that was very lively in most respects, but the worship was people-centred – we would sing a lot of songs about us and our love for God,' says Colin Owen.

'What Colin (Urquhart) has done for me in particular is to point me in the direction of God, namely we *proclaim* God in our praise. We proclaim His majesty, what He is, who He is, what He has done, His awesomeness, His goodness to us. We proclaim all these things and we proclaim them hard and loud and long!'

A 'people-centred' song tells God about the effect He has on us, which is the truth, but focuses the singers' attention on themselves. A typical song by Colin Owen is *Jesus you are mighty* which exalts Jesus and a particular facet of His nature.

Jesus you are mighty,
Jesus you're the King,
Jesus you are glorious,
And you rule everything.

The ruler of God's creation,
Because you are the Word,
Alpha and Omega,
The ever living Lord.

Who died and came to life again,
Who has the double-edged sword,
Alpha and Omega,
The ever living Lord.[1]

Colin Urquhart is not opposed to quiet worship, but over the years he has discerned that 'nice, quiet songs to get a sense of the Lord's presence' please the soul rather than stir the spirit, and he has instructed the worship leaders accordingly.

'Nice quiet songs are sung at the top of the mountain, not at the bottom,' he believes. 'We must climb the mountain in our praise to get a revelation of God's glory.'

There was actually a stage from November 1991 to October 1992 when very few slow, gentle songs were played. The decision was taken because of the general spiritual state at that time. Everyone loved God and wanted to draw near to Him, but to do so they needed to rise up in their praise, to ascend what seemed like a mountain in order to enter the holy of holies:

> 'Therefore, brothers, since we have confidence to enter the Most Holy Place by the blood of Jesus, by a new and living way opened for us through the curtain, that is, his body, and since we have a great high priest over the house of God, let us draw near to God with a sincere heart in full assurance of faith, having our hearts sprinkled to cleanse us from a guilty conscience and having our bodies washed with pure water.' (Hebrews 10:19–22)

Colin Urquhart teaches people that they must 'enter in' to God's holy and majestic presence if they are to worship in spirit and in truth. (John 4:24) Just sitting quietly is not entering in; we enter by speaking (or singing) our praises to God. Then we must enter in by faith, reminding ourselves if necessary that Jesus' blood has cleansed us from all sin; here some swift confession may be needed to clear away any obstacles to faith. This procedure helps ensure we are worshipping in faith and not in emotion.

He encouraged the worship leaders to concentrate on 'high praise', a Hebrew term meaning music which is high both in volume and pitch; it is intense and exuberant. When silences occur during high praise they are genuine; there is often a great deal of interaction between God and man taking place as worshippers remain lost in Him rather than thinking about lunch or someone's new jumper. Even singing in the Spirit can be just as loud as the praise, because the exuberance of high praise has brought the worshippers freedom as they have forgotten 'self'. Colin Owen has noticed that people's vocal ranges often expand when they sing songs either in English or in tongues inspired by the Holy Spirit at this point.

Convinced that God wanted to do a new thing in their worship, the musicians composed several warlike, spirit-stirring songs which proclaimed God's glory, splendour, majesty and power. The community loved them. They were sung often until the October 1992 week of revival meetings which, for many, were aptly named; the Kingdom Faith community and many visitors came closer in their personal lives to God's revival power. Once at that point, they felt led to sing slightly more subdued songs, but only for the reason that it was spiritually appropriate; many people had met with God in a new way and there developed what Colin called a 'sweetness' in the worship that he had been longing for ever since The Hyde revival. He knew that in real revival meetings musicians are a benefit but no longer necessary as everyone is meeting with God and praising Him spontaneously:

'In Wesley and Finney's time God managed to bring revival without P.A. systems.'

Nonetheless, the idea of worship is that we offer our

very best to God, which means the best equipment available to us today.

To anyone who queries the need for loud, upbeat music at Kingdom Faith meetings, Colin reassures them that it is preparation for heaven, a very noisy place according to the evidence in Revelation. God's voice is a trumpet, 'so if you like nice, quiet worship you'd better not plan to go to heaven!'

Colin Owen, a gifted instrumentalist married to worship leader Carol Owen, maintains it is up to us to conquer our feelings when we would prefer to sit quietly at the end of the day or in the early morning! 'The flesh needs to be told and shown its right and proper place, which is to be dead,' says Colin Owen firmly. 'It's the flesh that grumbles against praise, especially long, loud praise.'

So predictably it is the 'self', our flesh, which restricts our wholehearted worship, whether by emotions which dominate our spirit, or self-consciousness, which inhibits freedom of spirit and movement in worship by ensuring our attention is fixed on ourselves rather than on God.

Colin Owen feels there is a serious lack of teaching in British churches about worship in the Bible, despite the evidence of a king like David dancing in front of the ark of the covenant as he entered Jerusalem. (2 Samuel 6:16–23, 1 Chronicles 15:29)

He has seen that people will clap and lift their hands quite easily, 'but when it comes to dancing you hit a sticky patch in many churches'. After considerable research into biblical worship, from which he lectures Kingdom Faith students, he has no doubt that the Old Testament provides a solid scriptural basis for modern charismatic worship.

> 'Praise him with the sounding of the trumpet,
> praise him with the harp and lyre,
> praise him with tambourine and dancing,
> praise him with the strings and flute,
> praise him with the clash of cymbals,
> praise him with resounding cymbals.
> Let everything that has breath praise the LORD.'
> (Psalm 150:3–5)

Indeed, worship in King David's time must have been a cacophony of sound, with percussion (the resounding cymbals of Psalm 150 were as loud as gongs), stringed instruments, trumpet, tambourine and flute. There was also dancing, often in a chorus, from which we derive our modern interpretation of the chorus line dancing in unison.[2] And according to Revelation 5:11, heaven holds 'ten thousand times ten thousand' praising angels. ('The noise from that lot must make Concorde sound like a damp squib,' says Colin Owen.)

King David had a four-thousand piece orchestra providing an unimaginable volume of sound (1 Chronicles 23:5), while King Solomon had 120 priests playing the trumpet. (2 Chronicles 5:12) The sheer numbers show that in those days God's people were serious about praising their Lord and were not concerned about the decibels.

'You can't be quiet when you're joyful,' says Colin Owen. 'People who won't tolerate loud praise in church will go to a football match and they'll shout, scream and jump their praise! Why can't we do that for God?'

Research into Scripture led Colin Owen to believe that the devil had introduced the idea that loud praise was wrong, whereas the Bible shows it is loud and exuberant.

Logically, Satan is the one who least enjoys hearing God being loudly praised, having been expelled from heaven where he was worship leader.

Colin Owen and Jarrod Cooper, a worship leader and songwriter at Lamplugh House, agree that the problem with British worship is its false idea of dignity. When leading worship conferences, Jarrod encourages men to 'get out of manliness and into godliness'. Giving the example of King David dancing with all his might as he entered his city with the ark of the Lord, he points to the cost to 'self' of worship led by the Holy Spirit. David's wife Michal despises him, but he tells her that he will be even more undignified, and humiliated in his own eyes. In a telling adjoinder, we learn that Michal was barren to the day of her death. (2 Samuel 6:23)

Jarrod believes that there is opposition to dancing when

people are worried about appearing to dance in a worldly way which seems inappropriate in church.

'Satan doesn't want us to realise that our bodies are in subjection to the Spirit of God and they do what we tell them to do. So he'll bring in fear of what others will say, or, worst of all, will make you wonder if you're dancing in the right way!'

King David knew that, in Jarrod's words, 'he looked like a complete wally' and his people might dislike him, but he was offering a 'sacrifice of praise'. (Hebrews 13:15)

As a worship leader at Lamplugh House, Jarrod has the job of leading small groups of around thirty people in worship. When the team of eight people first arrived (to be joined later by up to twenty students), he could see they were all wondering how their worship would develop. Who would set the pace? And how great would the cost be as they were brought out of their 'comfort zones'?

'As worship leader I have to pay that cost,' says Jarrod, 'so I started dancing and exhorting them to get on with it. Very often I get up from the piano and dance now, so no-one can feel I'm getting off lightly! So we got through that embarrassment, which in any case is sin.'

Even now Jarrod will confront any student who is not joining in.

'I ask why they're not worshipping, because Jesus always confronted unbelief; it's loving to do so. The first thing Jesus said to His disciples after His resurrection was a rebuke – where was their faith?

'It's not nice having to rebuke people, but anyone in ministry who wants to be liked will end up in a rut.'

Everyone knows it is their shared responsibility to initiate worship as well as take part, which Jarrod encourages because he dislikes a 'platform mentality' where people expect to be spoon-fed from the front!

Non-Christians are not impressed, he asserts, by a church where people claim to love God but are determined to keep their dignity.

'They need to see there's a people living for someone so much greater than they are that they're willing to be 'humiliated' for His sake, giving all of themselves as they 'forget not all His benefits'. Worship is giving honour to someone so much greater that you suddenly don't care about yourself.'

Children of course love joyous music. Seeing a toddler tumbling around at the back of a meeting or waving a flag as big as himself gives particular pleasure at worship meetings, as does the sight of older children clapping or lifting their hands. 'Church' will not be a negative experience where they have to stand still. And babies rarely cry when they can contentedly bob about in their parents' arms. Having been free to dance about, the children usually sit quietly colouring or reading during the sermon on weekdays when there is no children's service.

In fact the children's worship will be similar to the adults'; the songs they sing at 'Faith Factory', Kingdom Faith's children's ministry, also proclaim biblical truth boldly with appropriate actions!

Anyone who is called to be 'up front' in a ministry is potentially vulnerable. This is as true of worship leaders as it is of preachers. Both can appear to have quite different personalities 'off-stage' when they are not ministering. Kingdom Faith worship leaders had to learn to resist sore throats, colds, and the enemy's insinuations, all directed at the area of their anointing.

'When you lead worship, God increases the anointing on you,' explains one of the Roffey Place worship leaders, who is quiet and reticent when not playing and singing.

'God tends to pick those who think they're inadequate. Like other worship leaders, I recently came to the point where I knew I was dead and had been crucified with Christ. This means you can write songs and have no pride when you hear people singing them. The Lord has to bring you to a place where you *believe* your flesh is dead and crucified and that His Holy Spirit lives in you. "I" don't matter – but it's something that has to be affirmed every day! It's no good having a revelation on Friday, living in it for the weekend and then from Monday onwards letting your feelings and circumstances tell you who you are rather than allowing God's word to tell you. If I start believing how I feel, I just say, "Sorry, Lord". All God sees when he looks at you is Jesus, like a pure white vessel.

'If you *are* dead to yourself, you're not bothered either about self-consciousness, because it's Jesus living in you who is the important one. What I look like and how I am doesn't matter. If people judge you, they're judging Jesus.

'To be honest, I don't much like leading worship, nor do at least two of the other worship leaders I know. But it's a calling so you have to do it. We're always learning, because the more you lead, the less you feel you know how to do it. We've all got L-plates on for the rest of our lives as far as learning is concerned!

'Obviously it's nice to be encouraged by the leaders sometimes, but I know that when I need approval it's because I'm moving away from my security in God. It really doesn't matter what people think if you've been obedient to God.'

Another, linked aspect of Colin's teaching which helped this young man was the decision not to look at how he felt. He realises that discouraging thoughts frequently come from the devil and admits that in the past his circumstances have seemed so burdensome that he has cried himself to sleep.

'The devil tends to attack you first thing in the morning, saying, "You're not in the mood to play so if you do, you'll be no better than a hypocrite". He can even suggest you're losing your anointing. That's why it's important to have the Spirit overflowing from you so you can tell the devil to get lost. God always gives you the strength to overcome, but you have to receive it by faith.

'If you are always looking at yourself, you feel as if it's you who's giving out all the time. And while most people can sit quietly at the back if they're feeling tired or they have some turmoil within themselves, the worship leader still has to be out at the front, having supposedly already met with God.'

He now believes that no matter how tired he feels, the Lord will give him the energy he needs. 'When we trust in Him and give Him our best, He gives us all we need. I came to the conclusion that because we have eternity with the Lord it doesn't matter if we feel tired now! If you accept the truth – that you're living in the Spirit –

you can receive all the strength you need. And where the flesh says, "You can't", God says, "You can".'

When actually leading worship, he knows he is not responsible for people entering into God's presence: 'That's between them and God. By choosing two or three songs to begin with, you're setting a sail for the Holy Spirit to move in and take over. It's great when it feels as if the Holy Spirit is blowing the worshippers into the presence of God.'

Despite these revelations he still feels nervous before he has to lead worship.

'There's a difference between nerves and fear, though. If you're fearful it means you're trying to do things in your own strength and you're not letting the Holy Spirit in. I feel nervous because I want to do what God wants. If nerves aren't there, you can be quite dangerous, actually. I've worked with over-confident musicians and it can be awful because they do their own thing without listening to the Holy Spirit.

'And, as the songwriter Chris Bowater discovered, the Lord tends to like you to feel a bit nervous because it keeps your eyes on Him.'

Another key aspect of leading worshippers into God's presence is to allow the music to flow from one song to the next continuously. This can last from fifteen minutes to an hour, depending on the Spirit's leading and the time it takes for everyone to stop being aware of their dignity and their feelings. Colin Urquhart gave his worship leaders instructions not to chat between songs like disc jockeys. Even earnest exhortations, let alone chirpy anecdotes, are a disruptive habit, interrupting the inner flow of worshipping hearts.

Being led by the Holy Spirit means that the worship leader cannot afford to let a congregation dictate what is played. 'You should never pander to a congregation; just give them what God's got for them,' declares Jarrod. 'It doesn't matter if you play a loud song when they want a quiet one because they're tired; we're not called to be "good" worship leaders but obedient ones.'

Worship leaders can slip into a habit of playing quiet 'worship songs' after two or three louder 'praise songs', whereas many worshippers may only be 'halfway up the mountain' at that point and will need longer to surrender their burdens to Jesus and enter into His holy presence. This is an active process as we draw near to God in our spirits. So there is a responsibility on worshippers to enter into the holy of holies for themselves.

'Don't expect the musicians to drag you in from the front,' said Colin Urquhart. 'It shouldn't be by their effort, but by your yielding to God's Spirit. Come with a sense of expectation and a hunger to meet with God again.'

Once in the holy of holies, our yielded spirits feel as if they are one with God's Spirit. We are privileged to experience God's perspective of us and our world, which may have been so burdensome even a few minutes ago. Aware of our insignificance before the throne of the One who names the stars, we delight to ascribe glory to God and affirm our willingness to do His will on earth as it is done in heaven.

'At once I was in the Spirit, and there before me was a throne in heaven with someone sitting on it.' (Revelation 4:2)

In God's awesome presence we marvel afresh that He took on human form and lived our life because He loved us so much. Now it is our turn to live His life, offering our bodies as a living sacrifice of praise, one part of our spiritual act of worship.

> 'Therefore, I urge you, brothers, in view of God's mercy, to offer your bodies as living sacrifices, holy and pleasing to God – this is your spiritual act of worship.' (Romans 12:1)

> 'Through Jesus, therefore, let us continually offer to God a sacrifice of praise – the fruit of lips that confess his name.' (Hebrews 13:15)

Chapter Nine

FIT TO SERVE

Gill Roll knew it was not God's plan for her to have cancer. Twice before she had been healed, yet this time it would have been so easy to give up hope. For the third time in her life cancer had attacked her body; this time the doctor was telling her she would die. It had begun at fifteen when she had had a kidney removed, followed in 1980 by an emergency hysterectomy operation.

From February 1988 to June 1989, cancer had affected one lung, her right arm and her neck, and she went blind in one eye. She was given only three months to live – and she was a member of a church which did not teach that God wanted to heal. Her own pastor, a Calvinist, did not believe the gifts of the Spirit were for today, so she visited another pastor whom she knew had faith for healing.

To all appearances she was in a sorry state; 'I'd been losing my hair and wearing wigs and was on my third session of chemotherapy which is the most you can have. But we prayed together and God just did it!'

She still had to face her disbelieving medical consultant who told her, 'Your God can't do it; you're only in remission.'

God had healed Gill's cancer, but she didn't get the sight back in her eye until the 1989 Kingdom Faith Camp. She had taken the wife of a church elder who was fifty-seven and suffered from epilepsy. Although her friend's husband was worried about his wife going away, he trusted Gill to look after her because Gill had experience of caring for her own daughter, Sarah, who was epileptic.

In the Thursday evening meeting Colin asked people who specifically knew God wanted to heal them to make themselves known. 'Come on, Gill, come forward with me,' her friend begged.

While Colin was praying for her friend, both she and Gill fell unconscious under the power of the Holy Spirit. When they got up, sight had returned to her eye. (Her friend had been healed of epilepsy, also, proved by the fact that she has suffered no further attacks.)

'I was expecting God to do it, but I didn't expect it then because I'd only gone forward with my friend because she had really thought God was speaking to her!'

In 1992, after three clear years, Gill was referred to her consultant again, this time with what she thought was kidney trouble. While awaiting test results, she went to a meeting in Ipswich held by John McKay where one of his team members brought a word of knowledge: someone at the meeting had 'cancer of the lower region'.

Gill did not react, as she did not believe the word was for her – until she returned to the hospital to hear that she had cancer again; this time it was in the liver. Her consultant was as negative as ever, bluntly telling her, 'I told you before you were in remission and your God couldn't do it. You'll never survive.'

It is always tempting for Christians to lose heart when they are 'seriously' ill, because they know dying will allow them to meet Jesus in His glory. But as a single parent with two of her own children and four foster children (three of whom had some form of disability), Gill knew that God did not want them abandoned.

Boldly, Gill contradicted the surgeon.

'That's not true. This time the cancer is in a totally different area.'

The consultant wanted Gill to go into hospital for an exploratory operation; she chose to postpone it until after her youngest daughter's wedding. Even after the wedding, she had no peace about the operation and telephoned Nicholas Rivett-Carnac at Roffey. After praying together over the telephone, Gill was convinced she should not have the operation. 'A barium meal had shown the cancer was in the liver; I could see no point in undergoing an operation just so they could tell me how long I'd got to live.'

Now Gill was completely on her own with God. Her stomach had distended so far that one of the Roffey students was to assume she was pregnant and her family nicknamed the lumpy tumour 'Fred'. Knowing there was no medical cure, she continued praying with faith, believing words from a psalm a friend had given her:

> 'The Lord is righteous in all his ways
> and loving towards all he has made.
> The Lord is near to all who call on him,
> to all who call on him in truth.' (Psalm 145:17–18)

Re-reading Colin's book, *Receive your Healing* and listening to his *Healing* tapes also helped: 'I think I listened to that first tape four times. Colin actually said on there that doctors cannot themselves heal; they can only help the healing process in the body. It is God who actually does it.'

So Gill opened her heart to God: 'All right, Lord, You don't want me to go into hospital because they're not going to do anything anyway. I'm going to rely on You. If You've got a job of work for me that You want me to continue, then You've got to do it for me.'

From then on she decided to trust God completely. Telephoning Nicholas again she asked, 'Will you stand in faith with me for my healing?' In his turn, Nicholas asked everyone at Roffey to stand with Gill too.

Two weeks after her daughter's wedding Gill went to a healing day led by Colin at Roffey.

During a time of ministry, Colin announced that someone had cancer of the liver. 'I knew that was me and so did everyone around me, so I just received that healing.'

Shortly after she returned home, the outward signs of cancer, jaundice and skin disorder, began to disappear, but 'Fred' was, if anything, growing. She was relieved about the jaundice disappearing because the children were becoming suspicious and her oldest daughter was due to take her nursing finals in two months' time. 'I hadn't said anything – it didn't seem right to worry them because I was trusting God to heal me. And I knew that Saturday that God had done it.'

It would be wrong to say that Gill never had any doubts about her healing, despite believing God's word and His willingness to heal her in the past. But Roffey was over one hundred miles away.

'I faltered, yes, because I had nobody at home to stand with me.'

A week after the healing day, she rang Nicholas again:

'I need to be around some folk with some faith.'

He arranged for her to stay at Roffey for two days. On the first day Nicholas and she prayed and waited on the Lord for over two hours and Gill felt her stomach beginning to shrink. Later that day, at the regular lunchtime prayer meeting, Nicholas felt it right for everyone present to lay hands on Gill. 'Talk about full of the Holy Spirit! I was so warm the rest of the day. Next morning I had my quiet time at about 3 a.m. and it had gone! I said, "Lord, you've taken it! Fred's not around any more!"'

Full of the good news, Gill had to contain her joy until breakfast when she could tell everyone what God had done for her. 'He's so majestic, and He keeps His promises.'

I first met Gill at Roffey the day after the healing day, when 'Fred' was still much in evidence beneath a loose-fitting dress. She looked pale and said grimly, 'I'm believing I've been healed, although I don't feel like it.'

Nine days later I met her again, just a few hours after her healing had manifested itself; now her stomach was perfectly flat and she was able to wear a slim-fitting pleated skirt. She was still radiant with joy, hardly able to believe what God had done for her, as she showed me nicely pink hands that were shedding the last signs of jaundice.

Through this experience, Gill learned to totally trust God. His repeated words to her were 'Trust me, child, trust me.'

These were the words she 'stood on' when all the physical signs confirmed the doctor's words and it could have seemed that her children would be motherless. 'I learned not to give in. I'd say to anyone sick that if you receive a healing, *know* you've received it, accept it, take it into you and continue praising God. I had to do that even when "Fred" was bulging and preventing me from praising God as I wanted to, and dancing.

'If you do falter and find self-pity coming in like I did, just get with somebody, on the phone or however, and pray in faith with them. I just knew God had done it and He was there, continuing to do it. It helped when two people at Roffey came up to me separately after the healing day and told me that they believed the Lord was just telling me to wait patiently. So that's what I had to do. I think the waiting was a lesson the Lord was teaching me – I can be quite impatient! And I came under a lot of attack from the enemy – but God's greater. Even praying with Nicholas, we knew that Satan was on the attack.'

Gill is still listening to her healing tapes and her faith for her dumb fourteen-year-old foster daughter's healing was rewarded when her daughter began to speak, despite having dysphasia, a condition in which the speech part of the brain fails to function.

'After coming to us, she became a Christian. She loves us to pray with her and read the Bible to her. She'll kneel down by her bed and talk to God – we can't understand it but God obviously does.'

'Faith working through love' needs to be seen particularly clearly in the healing ministry. Again and again Jesus healed where faith was operating to some degree; yet, as Colin frequently teaches, it is unloving to suggest to someone that they are not healed because their faith is insufficient: 'Such a remark reflects as poorly on the speaker as the sufferer.'

Healing is an area where it is far easier to teach from our own understanding rather than trusting in the Lord with all our heart and acknowledging Him in *all* our ways. (Proverbs 3:5–6) Some have even seen cases where leaning on one's own understanding literally proved fatal.

It seems sad that those who wish to promote Jesus' healing power at work today sometimes appear to be derided far more openly than those who, understandably, find it easier to soften the implications of God's promises, usually as a result of their own experience.

Colin's healing ministry was born after his ordination when he heard God telling him, 'Heal the sick.' At Luton his healing ministry became well-known; since then physical and emotional healings have been much in evidence as part of the 'signs following' his preaching. At Luton cases of illness fell dramatically as the church began to understand that sickness was of the devil and that they, as disciples of Jesus, had authority over all the powers of the enemy. 'The devil knew if he came round with any of that stuff he'd get sent packing.'

Deliverance itself is not over-emphasised in Colin's ministry, however. Years ago God told him, 'If you expect a fight with the enemy, you'll get one; if you expect victory, you will have victory.' So rather than have a spiritual tussle with demons, he will verbally take authority over the enemy if the Holy Spirit indicates that the disease, physical or emotional, has a particular demonic source. With the right authority, demons can be dismissed with a word as Jesus demonstrated.

Sometimes even an authoritative command is not necessary. A member of Kingdom Faith Church's pastoral team had been praying for the deliverance of a woman who had joined the church after experiencing many years of emotional and physical abuse at home. After praying for the woman at length, she saw her rush out of the Sunday morning service after the sermon. After a while the woman returned, sat with a friend who prayed with her, and afterwards was able to tell the pastoral team member that she was totally free. It was the result of hearing the word of God brought with authority and confirmed by a prophetic word from one of the congregation.

Colin learned, too, of the many ways through which God heals, from laying a hand on someone (without even necessarily praying) to letting God heal during worship:

> 'The corporate faith of believers joined in worship releases the power of God in ways not always experienced in personal ministry. Healing is the sovereign work of God, and during the past six years I have seen thousands healed from a great variety of diseases, healings that have stood the test of time.'[1]

Colin's healing ministry has developed more as the result of his concern to see people mature in their faith, than as a healing ministry for its own sake. His teaching on healing flows from his desire for everyone to have the right faith-love relationship with the Father:

'God delights to give to His children,' Colin told a healing conference. 'Don't you love to give to your children? I love being able to give to my kids, even though they're grown up. So you can see how much more God delights to give to us, His children.'

The people at that conference needed to receive a revelation about God's nature. Some of them needed to receive it for the second or third time because bitter experience had made them lapse into unbelief. Waiting to see God move could have made them doubt that it was God's will to heal them. Similarly Colin knew that many people could have been healed, as they had at other conferences and meetings he had led, but a proportion might lose their healings. If they knew, deep in their hearts, the extent of God's love for them and His desire to see it expressed in their lives, they would be better placed to receive and keep their healings. Deep assurance of God's love for them would leave no room for doubt and prevent their ever uttering again such prayers as:

'Lord, please heal him – if it is Your will.'

This version of Jesus' prayer in the Garden of Gethsemane does not belong in the healing ministry because it is used completely out of context. When Jesus prayed, 'Not my will, but yours be done' in the Garden of Gethsemane, He already knew the will of His Father. Crucifixion was inevitable for His Father's purposes to be fulfilled. His prayer is only appropriate when God is asking us to submit to something we do not like. But Jesus never prayed like that when ministering healing, because He *knew* it was His Father's will to heal.

God's will for healing is made clear in Isaiah's famous prophecy:

'Surely he took up our infirmities (sicknesses)
and carried our sorrows,
yet we considered him stricken by God,

smitten by him, and afflicted.
But he was pierced for our transgressions,
he was crushed for our iniquities;
the punishment that brought us peace was upon him,
and by his wounds we are healed.
We all, like sheep, have gone astray,
each of us has turned to his own way;
and the Lord has laid on him
the iniquity of us all.' (Isaiah 53:4–6)

Jesus has made full provision for healing on the cross, which we appropriate by faith. Colin believes that many people do not receive the healing God wants to give them because, deep down, they question whether God wants to heal them. When they pray, it is not with faith, with the confidence that this is the will of God, but they pray almost with a question mark. In other words, it is double-minded:

'But when he asks, he must believe and not doubt, because he who doubts is like a wave of the sea, blown and tossed by the wind. That man should not think he will receive anything from the Lord; he is a double-minded man, unstable in all he does.' (James 1:6–8)

The tragedy is that it is often the apparently thinking, Bible-believing intellectual Christians who allow their faith to be diminished by experience rather than relying, childlike, on a loving heavenly Father who has shown in His word and through His Son that He hates sickness. Sometimes we describe obstinate behaviour as 'childish', especially when someone refuses to bow to the 'superior' wisdom which is tempered by experience. Yet that is how we need to cling to God's word; with childish obstinacy we must hold fast to the assurance that He loves us and wants us to be whole in every way.

Faith for healing needs to rise above our experience and take hold of the supernatural, claims Colin.

'God wants us to believe that which is above the natural, even though often you only feel natural. You'll always find some people who tell you that's unreal. Are you telling me that there's anything more real than God, than His truth, His word? The things that people call real will pass away, but His word will endure forever. Now somebody can be sick with physical symptoms and say, "Well, the truth is, I'm sick." That's the truth *at the natural level.* The truth *at the supernatural level* is that by the stripes of Jesus they're healed. Now are they going to believe the natural or the supernatural, that which is over the natural?

'What many Christians believe lies in a halfway house. They believe the natural and they're trying to get the supernatural to change the natural. But when you really believe the supernatural, then it changes the natural.'

Once I was at a meeting where I talked with a gentle Spirit-filled lady who told me she was training to be a pastoral assistant. There were two other pastoral assistants in the diocese, a man with motor neuron disease and a woman with cancer. The man, she said, believed he would be healed but was getting visibly weaker. The woman was a 'mature' Christian who accepted 'whatever was God's will for her'.

I sometimes wonder if 'mature' in this context means 'resigned'. When Paul tells us he has learned to be content whatever the circumstances, he does not include sickness in his list of sufferings:

> 'I have learned the secret of being content in any and every situation, whether well fed or hungry, whether living in plenty or in want. I can do everything through him who gives me strength.' (Philippians 4:12b–13)

Paul's sufferings did not prevent his spreading the gospel; even in prison he wrote the valuable letters we have today. Any Christian confined to bed is not in a position to do everything, nor can we be expected to believe that God's strength is being made perfect in their weakness if that weakness is severe disabling illness rather than simply normal human limitations. Neither do Paul's other descriptions of physical suffering and trials (2 Corinthians 11:23–30 and 12:9) include illness in the list of persecution which resulted from his bold preaching of the gospel.

Although this lady had only been a Christian for three years, she had already been taught the usual arguments which are produced to attempt to show that healing is, to use Colin's expression, 'a divine lottery':

'What about Paul's thorn in the flesh?'

'What about that respected Christian leader who died in his prime?'

'Ah, but some people are called to sickness to glorify God.'

Mildly shocked, partly because we had just been praying for the healing of her husband's hearing, I managed to refute the arguments. Happily her husband already believed he would be healed and was able to remove his deaf aid when one of the ministry team prayed with him later.

Once home, I opened Colin's book *Receive your Healing*, and immediately found myself reading the section which answers all this lady's questions. Paul's 'thorn' is indeed a messenger from Satan:

> 'To keep me from becoming conceited because of these surpassingly great revelations, there was given me a thorn in my flesh, a messenger of Satan, to torment me.' (2 Corinthians 12:7)

This is how Colin explains Paul's 'thorn':

> 'The word translated as "messenger" appears 188 times in the New Testament. On 181 occasions the Greek word is translated "angel"; on the other seven the word "messenger" is used. On all occasions it refers to a person, never to an object or disease.
>
> 'In modern colloquial English we refer to a problematical person being "a pain in the neck" or "a thorn in my side". Elsewhere in the Bible the latter phrase is used to describe the enemies of God's people: "But if you do not drive out the inhabitants of the land, those you allow to remain will become barbs in your eyes and thorns in your sides. They will give you trouble in the land where you will live." (Numbers 33:55)
>
> 'It seems, therefore, that Paul was praying to God about someone who was opposing his work of proclaiming

> the gospel. We know from other references, including several in this same epistle, that Paul was constantly harassed by such opposition. Although he outlines many hardships faced, *nowhere does he include sickness among them.*'[2]

Faith for healing has to be active, not passive. It has to believe that God wants each of His children to be healthy; after all, how could they carry out Jesus' great commission to His disciples if they are ill at home, supposedly glorifying God in their sickness?

'Go into all the world and preach the good news to all creation. Whoever believes and is baptised will be saved, but whoever does not believe will be condemned. And these signs will accompany those who believe: In my name they will drive out demons; they will speak in new tongues; they will pick up snakes with their hands; and when they drink deadly poison, it will not hurt them at all; they will place their hands on sick people, and they will get well.' (Mark 16:15–18)

Jesus said, 'Heal the sick', not 'Pray for them'; He expects us to be a channel of His mercy. I admire those other 'mature' Christians for doggedly remaining Christian when they see God as a spiritual being who will apparently allow His children to suffer sickness without wanting to do anything about it.

I also found the answer to this lady's second query. When people perceived as powerful men and women of God are not healed, it can be because they have faith for salvation but not for healing. Some great evangelicals, rightly loved by thousands, fall into this category.

Believing in a God who will 'allow' illness only to magnanimously heal it so He can receive the glory is to reduce Him to the level of an uncaring despot; it is both illogical and inconsistent. Both Colin and Dan have shown the futility of this position by taking it to its logical conclusion: 'This is the good news. God gives blindness, makes people deaf, gives out cancer, pneumonia – come and follow Jesus!'

Exercising a healing ministry cannot be separated from the rest of our Christian lives. Colin believes that many Christians put their Christian lives into compartments, listening keenly to God for, say, their healing ministry, anxious to get every word from Him that will help those to whom they are ministering. But they are less keen to listen in other areas – in fact, it may not even have occurred to them to listen to God in these areas. This omission affects their authority in healing; God sees us as a whole, not broken down into ministries.

Too often it is the apparent failures which remain in the minister's mind. During a South African tour in 1980, Colin saw the Holy Spirit fall on six thousand people at one meeting. Countless people were being healed. Yet one of Colin's chief recollections was of praying for a black boy with a tumour who was not healed there and then. Happily he saw the black boy well again three evenings later. Similar encouragement came twelve years later in May 1992 when he received a letter about a brain-damaged young man for whom he had prayed during that visit twelve years earlier.

'The boy's father informed me that his son had been completely healed and had just graduated as an electronics engineer!'

As a government official with access to top politicians, he now wanted forty copies of Colin's book *Anything You Ask* to send to each member of the South African cabinet!

In fact, when Colin had prayed about that delayed healing in South Africa he felt that God was telling him there needed to be more power and authority in his ministry; 'You need to grow in faith'. He realised immediately that there is no room for complacency in the ministry of the Holy Spirit, although God did continue to encourage him with His gracious healings of others in the meantime.[3]

Ray McCauley could also have been daunted by apparent failure to heal people. In his first week as a minister two people he prayed for died. His response? 'Next, please!'

He points out that surgeons don't hang up their scalpels every time a patient dies. In the same way that a percentage of deaths does not invalidate their training and skill, so the fact that sick people sometimes die does not mean that God does not wish to heal nor that the minister should cease praying with the sick.

Although God will graciously heal us when we have little faith, we are still expected to grow up and reach a stage where we can stand on our own feet as mature disciples. This has always been Colin's aim in his ministry. He is keen for Kingdom Faith Church members to develop their own faith as soon as possible. It has not been easy because many needy people arrived from places where they felt their needs were not being met. Colin was perturbed to find that the same people kept coming forward for prayer.

'When we pray for people, things *need* to happen. And if they don't, either we're not in the faith or we're not moving by faith at that moment or we shouldn't be praying for them at that moment.'

After he prayed about it, God reminded Colin of a simple truth. In the gospels, there are *no incidents when Jesus prayed with any of His disciples to be healed.* As we read in Matthew 4, what the gospels constantly affirm is that people were brought to Him *out of the crowd*, the unsaved, like the woman with the haemorrhages, the centurion, the paralysed. Colin realised that the disciples either never got sick, or were healed in some other way.

In over thirty years of healing the sick, it had always struck him how much easier it was to heal unbelievers or new Christians than those who were further on in their faith.

'As I travel around I see dozens, sometimes hundreds healed at a single meeting. The power of God just moves in. We could say, why don't we have a move of God like that every Sunday so we get similar results every Sunday? It's different being out in ministry, in evangelism and conferences, than ministering to the same people week by week by week in the church situation.'

He saw that while Jesus healed the crowds who came to Him, He *taught* the disciples, because faith comes from hearing the word of God.

'Jesus was very happy to meet those who came to Him at the point of faith that they had. He asked them questions to draw out that faith: "Do you believe that I am able to do this?" And of course their faith level would have risen no end because they were seeing people getting healed around them. That happens at our Faith Camp every year – you see crutches being thrown away and everyone gets excited.'

With the disciples it was different. By *teaching them the word* constantly, Jesus was putting into their lives a deposit of faith that first of all would show them how to resist sickness and secondly, if they got sick *they would be able to come to the Lord themselves in faith.*

Jesus' principles for every generation of disciples encompassed things they had to do for themselves:

1) They had to *believe*: 'Everything is possible for him who believes.' (Mark 9:23)

2) They had to *speak* to their 'mountains' of need and see them move – without doubting in their hearts! (Matthew 17:20)

3) They could *agree* together by joining their faith (Matthew 18:19–20)

Thus their faith was in the word itself – not in the service, not in a particular ministry, not in a moment of time, but *in the word.* So when, for example, Jesus cast seven demons out of Mary Magdalene or ministered to others who came to Him for help, it was in order that they could then minister to Him in love.

'Healing isn't some kind of holy pot luck, where if you get prayed with enough, bingo! If we taught Jesus' principles in our churches, we wouldn't have healing lines with little happening.'

In this key message Colin was exhorting his church to become more like Jesus' disciples, to have the faith of someone like Gill Roll. He knew too well that some people go from one healing meeting to another, saying to themselves, 'Ah, so and so's preaching there. I'll try him. Oh, here's a visiting preacher. It's always more powerful with a visiting preacher because we're used to the same old voices again and again!'

If a church is to be a New Testament church, it needs to reach the place where miracles are happening every week, not necessarily in the service or even in life groups, but in supernaturally natural ways where everyone will hear how God is undertaking for His people in their daily lives.

An example of healing without a lot of fuss happened for a young man in the church who had broken his arm. When he went to have the plaster cast changed, an X-ray showed that the bone was whole again.

Another incident which has become part of Roffey folklore occurred when Pam Hunt's hand was crushed in a food mixer. A nurse on the team diagnosed several broken fingers; the pain was excruciating. Colin was called to pray for her and she managed, unbelievably, to sleep for two hours. When she awoke, her hand was completely restored.

All the team at Roffey are compassionate towards sickness; in the past the ministry may have been accused of having a black and white attitude to physical healing, but in fact it is only a minority of students who cause any guilt in the sick person. When this happens, it is from the most well-meaning motives such as when an enthusiastic young African slapped various flu sufferers on the back, jarring their grinding flu headaches, and pronounced, 'You are healed, brother/sister.'

It should be emphasised that Colin himself has a more pragmatic approach:

> 'Some people have been hurt by a mistaken interpretation of Jesus's words: ". . . believe that you have received it, and it will be yours" (Mark 11:24), particularly in the realm of healing. There are those who assert: "As soon as you have prayed, you are healed! Ignore all the symptoms and pain, and exercise your faith!"
>
> 'Sometimes people are advised to discharge themselves from hospital, to stop all medical treatment, get out of their sick-beds and behave as if they were healed. It is not difficult to imagine the disastrous consequences that can result from such advice.
>
> 'The promise is: "it WILL be yours". Jesus does not say that it will be yours *immediately*. He does not tell us to perform acts of foolhardy bravado to try to prove that we believe and that we are trusting Him. In fact, if anything, such acts indicate a lack of faith. It seems that people who adopt such an approach are not

> prepared to trust God to honour His promise in the way that He decides, at the time that He knows is best.
>
> '. . . if the sick person refuses, or obeys but has to take to his bed again, he is merely told: "You don't have the faith, brother!"
>
> 'As Christians, we are to forgive such unloving spiritual blundering. It is not easy always to do so. It doesn't seem to occur to such people that, if they are involved in the situation, their own faith is just as much at stake. A pertinent question can be asked of them: "Do you have the faith and authority to address the mountain and see it moved?"'[4]

Naturally it is not a good idea to ignore the requirements of your body; one should ensure adequate sleep and keep one day a week as a sabbath, a day of rest and worship. Sickness is certainly *not* God's will for any of us, but He will still triumph in the situation if we let Him do so. This does not mean that God 'sends' illness to teach His children a lesson, an idea Colin finds particularly repellent. 'After all, what loving earthly father would wish a dose of flu on his child because it needed to learn, say, patience?'

Colin knows the importance of people being relaxed in order to receive healing, and will often tell someone a joke before praying for them. At a physically low time it is so easy for one's spiritual well-being to be affected, too. One girl had come to Roffey as a student after holding down a high-powered civil service job and was used to working a ten-hour day. It is very hard to abandon the world's idea of an achieving lifestyle, and the big lesson she learned was to 'abide' in Jesus. 'I've got to stop striving,' she would say.

So Christians, like Jesus' disciples, need to become mature, in the sense of letting a strong faith emerge from a close, loving relationship with God. Then, like Peter's mother-in-law, they can get on with ministering to others.

Like physical healing, emotional healing must also be appropriated by faith. In the process, however, there may be a lot of cleaning out necessary, as the Holy Spirit brings up past unconfessed sin, such as unforgiveness. It is the way we then respond to the past which determines whether the pain lessens or stays raw. Often we need a revelation that Jesus has taken *all* our pains on the cross, both physical and emotional.

The metamorphosis resulting from learning new reactions is seen many times in Kingdom Faith students and church members. Some arrive with excess emotional baggage – recent or buried events and hurts which need to be resolved before they can move forward in faith.

If too troubling to be dealt with in solitary prayer, they can have a pastoral session of prayer with Nicholas Rivett-Carnac, the pastor, who often works with his wife Marigold.

The availability of Nicholas and Marigold is invaluable; their graciousness and unceasing interest in new students provides a model of pastoral ministry.

While Colin introduces what to many is the new concept of believing what God says over and above our personal feelings and circumstances, it is all too easy at the beginning, while the balance is being readjusted, to slip up and react emotionally to circumstances! At that point students book an appointment with Nicholas. If it is only a temporary blip and unlikely to need the tissue box, he can be caught over morning coffee or at the dining-table.

Dwelling on the past, whether living on past blessings or allowing oneself to be absorbed by past problems, will not help usher in revival, and for this reason Colin has become incensed with some of the Church's counselling methods which allow people to keep talking about their past. They are attempts to heal the soul, whereas our whole 'self' has already been crucified if we accept the truth. 'These methods have become a curse on the Church, preventing people from moving forward,' Colin maintains.

As far as he is concerned, one outpouring of self-pity should be enough. At Luton a former pop star had started coming to St Hugh's. Having quite a past, it was now burdening him. He got into the habit of coming to the vicarage and offloading his problems onto Caroline. After she had listened for a few times to the same things, she said to him, 'You need to repent.'

Colin always points out that Jesus told His disciples to heal the sick – not to pray for or counsel them! He believes people often seek counselling because they are not aware of all that Jesus promises.

Jesus said, 'The truth will set you free,' which means, since Jesus is the way, the truth and the life, that He is the answer. For years Colin has sought to teach people to understand the nature of their new identity in Christ and to 'live in the good of your new nature because you are a new creation. The old has gone and the new has come for anyone who is in Christ'.

His response to wrong counselling methods has been to produce his own course, *Direct Counselling*, which has proved to be a very popular subject for conferences. While many of us undoubtedly find it comforting to talk about ourselves to someone sympathetic, and 'get it off our chests', talking does not provide a permanent solution. Faith does.

Nor is Colin being at all arrogant in his opposition to what he terms 'pseudo-psychological methodology' infiltrating the Church. If he were lacking in compassion, he and Caroline would have closed their doors to some of the needy people who came to them for prayer over the years. As it was, the only answer for many was to take them into their own home to live as part of a normal family. Through being obliged to listen to people talking about their problems at length, Colin has learned that it is only the truth, the living word, which sets people free.

A daily diet of the truth and plenty of loving acceptance helped one young girl come through to wholeness in Christ. Sharon Pearce is one of the bounciest members of the Lamplugh House team. Small, blonde and pretty, she is almost always laughing.

Hers was a dramatic conversion, both in terms of becoming a Christian and of changing from a morose, scornful teenager who felt life had treated her badly, into the joyful person she is today.

In September 1990 she wandered into one of the

Tuesday night open meetings at Roffey, intending to have a laugh at her Christian friends' expense. Since the age of fourteen, her search for love had led her to try alcohol and drugs. She favoured the 'Gothic' look and dressed totally in black, with fierce dyed black hair and exaggerated pallor. 'I dressed in black, and there was darkness all round me. I wanted to be normal, but I didn't know how to be. Nothing I tried satisfied me. I couldn't do the average nine-to-five job. I was moving on every two weeks, stealing from shops and ripping off mail order catalogue companies to survive.'

Once in that meeting, she became more aware than ever of the hopelessness of her existence but could see no way of getting out of it. Back at her temporary home in Portsmouth, she was about to get involved in drug-dealing, but spoke to God first: 'Lord, I really want to get out of this mess and have a new life, but everywhere I move there's somebody trying to pull me into the drugs scene. If you really want me, Lord, you've got to pull me out.'

She started travelling in to Roffey each day for meals. 'People were really praying for me, though I didn't know it at the time.'

No suitable job was found for Sharon, and every possible Christian home fell through. In the end someone spoke to Colin about her, who prayed and discerned that God wanted Sharon to be at Roffey.

At first it was the love and encouragement which kept Sharon at Roffey. To her surprise, the people didn't go off her after a few weeks, so Sharon decided to seek God for herself.

'God just started to change me, bit by bit. After a few weeks, God just came in. At night, I kept meeting with Him in an amazing way. People were patient with me, they just loved me through all the problems.'

One night, she could not sleep. 'What's going on, God?' she asked.

'I want you to throw away your Gothic clothes and jewellery,' was the reply. 'Will you do that for Me?'

It was a battle for Sharon because she had to admit that her security lay in the bells round her neck and the bangles on her arms. She could hide behind her outrageous façade.

'As I threw the stuff away, God changed part of my character. Bit by bit He kept doing that. So from the hurt, rejected person who was always flying off the handle and couldn't do a thing, He made me strong.'

Although she told no-one of her decision, next day various people felt led to give her clothes. Suddenly she looked like a normal teenager in jeans.

From then on, Sharon was completely open to the Holy Spirit and has been used to minister powerfully to others. 'He started to encourage me by using me in miraculous ways, in healings and prophecy. I still struggled with giving up things, like smoking, but every time I gave up something, He blessed me back. Everything that's been stolen from my youth has been given back to me; I have a family now.'

In the daytime Sharon helps cook for the team and students at Lamplugh House; in the evenings and on mission she is being used increasingly to minister to others. Her previous interest in the occult has been more than adequately replaced by the Holy Spirit's gifts. Now she receives words of knowledge and discernment which she has used in healing and describes as 'really *fun*'.

Sometimes she gives a message from the Lord at a meeting and recently has been called to pray with people in pastoral situations. She cannot believe how much God has done in and through her:

'I know that none of it's me, and there are still so many areas where I need to become more like Christ, to be more loving.'

Her awareness of being privileged ensures that God can use her. 'You bow down to God, and He raises you up and lets you do great stuff.'

Yet she is also an ordinary teenager, who had collected more hurts and emotional scars than young people from more sheltered backgrounds. Nor is she immune to memories, but has learned how to deal with them.

'If there's something I struggle with, where I think, "Lord, this isn't glorifying to you", then I give it to God. Even if it's a big problem, I know God will sort it out. And it doesn't have to take long – you just go for it.'

When she is feeling low, she confesses it and God reminds her not to listen to her feelings. 'That's not faith – I'm a new creation and I can just forget about the past. That's all there is to it.'

By using her will to bring problems to God, and believing He has dealt with them, Sharon now feels as if her past happened to another person. 'I just feel like a normal person now, except I'm really going for God.'

Someone like Sharon is ready for revival. At nineteen, she has left an unhappy past at the cross, so God has been able to turn her life around.

Healing should not supersede other aspects of ministry; it is thrilling to see people being healed, but the important part is that they are now fit to serve the King. As one leader with a strong healing ministry said, 'God didn't set you free to watch television.'

Chapter Ten

A PEOPLE OF POWER

'For it is by grace you have been saved, through faith – and this not from yourselves, it is the gift of God – not by works, so that no-one can boast. For we are God's workmanship, created in Christ Jesus to do good works, which God prepared in advance for us to do.' (Ephesians 2:8–10)

These verses sum up the interesting tension between those 'good works' which on their own are not a ticket to heaven and those which God expects of Christians, including the great commission to go out into all the world, healing the sick, casting out demons and teaching them Jesus' commands. (Matthew 28:19, Mark 16:15–18)

The key is in being 'in Christ Jesus' and operating in obedience to His leading and His word. And we have the help of the Holy Spirit.

If the charismatic movement deserves criticism, it is for its tendency to concentrate on the 'me and God' experience, its failure to siphon off God's gracious outpouring of His Spirit in the direction of others. A well-known teacher and writer with a strong prophetic ministry commented that Western Christianity had become selfish: 'New Testament Christianity is *not* a privatised religious experience culminating in the great cop-out of the rapture. This is an invention of Western individualism: Lord, please look after me and my family (and to hell with everyone else).'

Colin says something rather similar: 'God didn't put you on earth for a picnic.'

He wants to see Christians leave behind their charismatic ideology and move into what he terms 'revival ideology', so that their goal is not simply to be filled with the Holy Spirit, but to walk in the Spirit, with all His attendant power, love, grace and mercy. Dan Chesney has said, 'If tongues were all you looked for when you were baptised in the Holy Spirit, you've missed the point. Jesus wanted His disciples to know they'd received *power* to go out as His witnesses to the ends of the earth. God anoints us to go, not to hug the anointing to ourselves.'

Colin believes that the Church is actually guilty of pride if it fails to expect signs to follow its evangelism of non-believers. For those outside the Church, the outworking of Christ's life is most likely to be seen in individual church members. There's the popular expression, 'You're the only Bible some people will ever read'.

Prayer and evangelism

Studying the early Church's evangelism methods was a breakthrough in understanding for many Kingdom Faith students. They returned to the great truth that evangelism happened naturally because the disciples were living in the power of the Holy Spirit when miracles seemed to be a daily occurrence. They had followed Jesus, were submitted to Him and now continued to do what they had seen Him doing. Ray McCauley once said that the Book of Acts is a blueprint for personal revival.

An example of modern-day evangelism with the Holy Spirit's power came from a former Kingdom Faith lecturer, Andrew Shergold; he himself had lived for a year in revival power when praying for people's healing was frequently part of evangelism, or evangelism resulted from healing, with the results sometimes surprising even the evangelist! A Muslim woman he was working with in Harrods' toy department had a damaged hand, so Andrew boldly told her, 'Jesus can heal your hand.'

When the lady took him at his word and asked him to pray, he was completely taken unawares. Uncertain that his prayer would be effective, he asked the lady to come to the stock-room away from the shop floor because he expected to be embarrassed publicly. He started praying to Jesus, not really sure of what to say, when the woman said, 'Stop! My hand was healed as soon as you said "Jesus".'

Later, Andrew saw the woman in the staff cafeteria in the centre of a group of other Muslim women, telling them, '. . . and this Jesus healed my hand!' Evangelism was taking place just as the good news spread in Jesus' time.

The use of prayer before and during evangelism yielded powerful information. Students travelling with Colin saw the benefit of two hours' prayer before a meeting or outreach because they would receive words of knowledge and pictures of the people they were going to meet. Mike Skelton, the pastor of the King's Fellowship, Ramsgate, a church affiliated to Kingdom Faith, taught his congregation to rely heavily on the Holy Spirit, as well as fasting to drive out stubborn areas of unbelief in evangelism. 'Christians go out in fear, not faith, instead of expecting God to have prepared people,' he declared.

Having done a limited amount of street evangelism, I was used to praying beforehand, assuming that half an hour showed we were pretty serious. Trying to tell strangers about Jesus was still a nerve-wracking and sometimes discouraging experience, however, and understandably not the most popular activity amongst almost all the Christians I knew.

My experience of street evangelism with really serious prayer, however, proved that not only would we talk to the right people whose hearts were ready to hear the gospel, but that we would have courage and confidence. In other words, it was not too far from fun!

Before a group of students set off for street evangelism, we spent a good half hour worshipping God, getting our focus back onto Him after our other activities. We sang more than we prayed. Naturally it could be argued that we were getting 'hyped up', but I see it more as an army doing last-minute training exercises, reaffirming our beliefs before we conveyed them to others. And there was no doubt we had a real sense of God's Spirit; on one occasion we were also encouraged by two prophecies from our intercessors who told us separately of God's pleasure at our willingness to do this work for Him.

The whole time we were out, a group of four intercessors prayed constantly for us, literally battling in the spirit for souls. Out on the street, we were astonished at the openness of the people we felt directed to approach. I had never experienced such willingness to talk about personal beliefs – it could only have been the result of prayer. On one occasion, two of the pairs had conversations with people that led to their praying to Jesus and wanting to make a commitment to Him. When we returned, we discovered the results had been expected by the prayer group. Just before the people came through to praying, the intercessors had felt compelled to intensify their efforts, labouring in the spiritual realm to bring two souls to new birth. 'I was in travail,' said one, 'and afterwards my tummy ached, just as if I'd given birth.'

Another time I witnessed this was before a major outreach by Kingdom Faith Church in its local town of Crawley. I had been to Crawley before – and was struck by the heaviness of the atmosphere. There was high unemployment and in the town square many shops were trying in vain to lure hard-up customers with 'Sale' signs. On the morning of the outreach the church assembled in the town square ready to worship God in music and perform two drama sketches. So often in that situation Christians can feel self-conscious, aware they are in a minority, wondering if they will be fed to the lions. That morning it was different; the lions were disarmed.

The moment I stepped into the square my spirit lifted; *it was just like going into one of the church meetings*. There was a lightness, joy and anticipation in the atmosphere which made it easy to pray, to sing, clap and dance. A while later I discovered the reason; two of the team, committed to the evangelism programme, had been up since midnight praying. The heavens were well and truly cleared. That day eight people came to Christ – there was even an enquiry about where they could get a copy of the music! In times of revival, conversions are of course higher, but that morning the church was encouraged, even elated. On such outreaches the church members know it helps to attend in large numbers; twenty people are far less impressive worshipping God than two hundred people.

Conversions made during revival are known to last, because there is thorough, deep repentance. Sometimes Christians are so keen to emphasise the love of Jesus that they diminish His holiness. 'Come to Jesus, He's waiting with His arms held out' is something many of us have said. As Charlie Brown, a Christian for thirty-eight years who combined prison ministry and carpentry on the Kingdom Faith team said, 'We can imply they're doing Jesus a favour. And if you're doing someone a favour, you can withdraw it at any time. But a drowning man isn't going to chuck away the rope you throw him.'

Colin realised there was a difference in the quality of conversions today compared with those in times of great revival. Wesley and Finney did not consider someone truly converted until they had repented fully by deciding no longer to live for themselves but to live 'the Christ life'. People agonised over this decision for days and weeks sometimes, literally in an agony of soul. And they had no inner peace until they made their decision for Christ, which meant far more then than it does in its twentieth-century usage.

To Wesley, a backslider was someone who had slidden back from their total commitment to Jesus. In other words, they expected what the New Testament expects of Christians.

After reading of these men's exploits for God, Colin asked Him if modern evangelists had learned anything new.

'No,' he was told. 'In those days they did the job properly.'

This is also one of the reasons Colin holds out little hope for the work of the lone evangelist. 'It's not much good having people wander up to the front of a meeting and "making a commitment" if there's no real repentance. We need to get people saved, baptised in the Holy Spirit, and duck 'em quick! I'm looking forward to the day when the baptistry pool will be permanently open. When God moves, it won't be twenty a year or even twenty a month, but twenty a week, every week, getting baptised.'

Dan Chesney has experienced the problem of few 'stayers' after conducting large evangelistic crusades for churches in America. Once in Britain, he evangelised in pubs with rock bands, on the streets, on barges, in parks, concerts and churches. 'One morning I had four hours – a whole morning – in a comprehensive school helped by a fifteen-piece band. At the altar call two hundred kids *ran* to the front. In six years I've seen thousands of people come to Christ, but I had a sense of dissatisfaction at the low staying rate. What was I building?'

Similarly, it was hard for the Bethany Fellowship to sustain the ministry needed by the people who came to The Hyde seeking it, because they had no church. 'Mistakes were made because people went too fast, they were so full of fire and enthusiasm,' says Colin.

Both men have seen how conversions happen in times of revival. Immediately after God's revival power visited The Hyde as the result of five weeks' intensive prayer, Colin and his team toured Britain conducting Kingdom Faith crusades. There were extraordinary happenings, as if at every meeting God wanted to give them a fresh reminder that He and He alone was in sovereign control of events. One hour for prayer before the meetings became totally inadequate – they would stretch to two hours as the team sought God. Time and again Colin saw the truth of his discovery that whatever happens in the prayer meeting will be reproduced in the main meeting. As for the team, the first thing they inspected on arrival in a new building was the floor quality – because they knew they would be spending most of their time face down on it.

Once the meeting started, the team was forbidden to comfort people in distress unless the Holy Spirit gave them permission. 'No-one needed counselling,' said Colin, 'because God did the ministry. People wept their way through to God.'

Dan saw revival conversions in America before his call to England. He believes his ministry was born during a three-month period when he lived in revival. He was praying for six to eight hours a day, in prayers guided by the Holy Spirit. 'If you do this, you change radically because you literally begin to experience death and resurrection. I personally entered into revival because the Holy Spirit *is* revival.'

In his church he started prayer groups. 'Fifteen came at first – five of them were unsaved. We prayed in the Spirit for one hour. The five broke down, but no one saw to them because they were caught up in the Spirit. After fifteen minutes the five stood up and prayed in tongues also! They were converted – *by God*.

'So we had a prayer meeting every night after that and people got saved because that's how God wanted to do it that time. People brought unsaved friends because they knew the power of God would be there. The new converts came back every night; after a week they were on-fire evangelists!'

This went on for eighteen months before the revival power waned. 'Perhaps this was due to me,' said Dan, 'but it's touched me for ever.'

One potential danger he saw at that time was that of pride in what God was doing amongst them:

'You can't have pride in your anointing because it's from the Lord. But there's nothing wrong with seeking Him for more so He can use you more fruitfully.'

After meeting a South American whose country was experiencing revival in 1992, Michael Barling brought back the wisdom that there are three elements essential to sustaining revival: vision, anointing – and humility. In that country, large churches seemed to spring up almost overnight, only to shrink in less than a few years.

Colin agrees that feeling proud about what God is doing amongst a body of His people is the fastest way to lose revival. 'If you don't walk humbly, and start to think all that God's doing is your doing, the show's over.'

What both Colin and Dan learned from the way God graciously touched their lives was that revival made evangelism simple. Flowing naturally from what God was doing, it was not a burden.

'Revival has always been the fruit of prayer in my life,' says Colin, who is increasingly aware of God calling him to sacrifice other aspects of his work to spend time in prayer. 'In Luton we were a praying church. We just lived and breathed prayer – and people came. After eighteen months we had (which was then unique) a congregation of Spirit-filled people. This birthed a great burden for evangelism. But we learned that if you don't get the strategy from God you're wasting your time. God's word to us was "Love one another that the world will know you are My disciples." So we had to learn what it meant to lay down our lives for one another. The fruit of that? People just came.'

A popular method of prayer at Kingdom Faith services is for people to hold hands in a chain of prayer. At St Hugh's, Luton, this was one of the ways by which many came to know the Lord and were filled with the power of the Holy Spirit, while Kingdom Faith services usually see several new Christians. Colin did not encourage visitors from other churches to stay at St Hugh's. 'They had to return, healed and Spirit-filled, to their own churches as witnesses.'

The new Kingdom Faith Church has already been criticised for attracting members of other local churches, although it primarily seeks to and is filling its seats with new converts. He is also concerned that other ministers with 'successful' churches should not be discouraged by such criticism; other local churches and their ministers are prayed for at Kingdom Faith prayer meetings.

But if people stray into Kingdom Faith Church because they like the look of the pasture, they may realise they were more comfortable grazing quietly elsewhere. Since its birth, Colin and Dan realise that God has been leading their church through a process of revival where nice 'experiences' of God give way to the urgency of doing God's real work. What concerns God is His goal, which should be our goal. The route to that goal is not so important, He led Colin to believe; there might be exciting spiritual experiences for some and not for others, but experiences were not a part of revival.

In no uncertain terms, God laid His goal before Colin in October 1992, when the church was less than a year old. Its challenge was so great that Colin realised he could not have put it to the Kingdom Faith community earlier.

'My goal,' God told him, 'is that everyone of My children will choose to live the Christ life.'

This was the first time God had used the term 'Christ' to Colin; usually He referred to His Son as 'Jesus'. Immediately obvious was that 'Christ' means 'the anointed One'. Knowing 'the anointing breaks the yoke of the oppressor', the equation was clear: when Christians determine to live the anointed life of Christ, the yoke of oppression is broken and we move into proper revival.

'For to me, to live is Christ and to die is gain.' (Philippians 1:21)

This revelation convinced Colin that it is only those living the Christ life who will bring revival to the nation. The key? Submission to God. Colin stressed that God does not intend the Christian life to be a constant struggle to overcome the self.

'The only way is to stop fighting that which is negative and submit those parts of yourself to Christ, so you reflect Jesus in that area of your life, whether it's love, faith, or another fruit of the Spirit. (Galatians 5:22) What you don't yield to Jesus, the enemy will try to take, so the fight goes on.'

He believes too many Christians hold on to 'self', wanting to be in control of their lives. They pray to God to help them in what they will do, rather than submitting completely to Him so He can work through them. Before preaching, for example, Colin prays, 'Lord, please flood my soul, spirit and body with your love, peace and joy.'

When he needs more 'help' during the day, he simply submits himself afresh to God.

Someone else who saw the fruit of submission to God was a student at Lamplugh House, who went through a time of seeking and submitting to God with the rest of the team and students. Typically he was not aware of what God had done in him during that time, until he went to speak to a businessmen's dinner. Later he reported incredulously that twenty people had become Christians and two women were healed of disabilities.

The Christ life will, as previously stated, be evident in our attitude to one another. For this reason much Kingdom Faith Church growth is expected to take place through its 'life groups', known in many churches as 'home' or 'house' groups.

Each of the fourteen original groups of between nine and twelve people had a target of doubling by the end of their first year. However, Colin stressed that this was not a target to strive at: 'If you think, "We must evangelise", it won't work,' he told the leaders. 'We need a move of God in the groups and then it will happen just like that.'

Many who had joined the church from within a twenty-five mile radius had great needs. They were bringing with them family and home problems which had persisted for years, whittling away their faith; problems which Colin described as 'horrendous in the natural realm'. He is keenly aware of the church's responsibility to do more than help people cope with their situations; its members are to see others' problems resolved and lives transformed.

It is at this point that the church's pastoral structure will be tested. Dan and Colin want every church member to be as spiritually mature as possible; this means being fully equipped to pray for anyone's needs, whether they be for provision or healing, without wanting to refer every matter to the pastors. In a church of hundreds, let alone thousands, that is clearly impossible.

Therefore the life group must provide initial pastoral care. People who need special help, such as those who have been heavily involved in the occult or drug abuse, can be referred to one or two pastoral leaders who have experience of helping such people. But the purpose is for most problems to be dealt with at 'local level'. In this way faith is built up amongst church members as they see God moving in the lives of those they have prayed for. As Colin says, 'The real test of faith isn't having faith for yourself and your own needs, but for others' situations.'

The geography of the area means that some life groups consist almost entirely of needy people, which presents a particular challenge for the group leaders as they seek to build up the faith of their members.

God's people must be active in evangelism not only because they have had a revelation about the millions going to hell, but because God wants to build enormous churches in the coming years! 'The day of big churches is coming,' says Colin. 'Why? Because God's interested in size? Yes. Get rid of that thinking that small is beautiful. Big churches can do ministry that small churches can't.'

He believes that the reason God wants to build big churches is to accommodate the extra numbers who will be pouring into His Kingdom. This will be achieved by the climate in the nation changing, once the yoke of spiritual oppression is broken by those living the Christ life.

The responsibility for revival is not solely in the hands of a few anointed leaders in strategic places around the country, but in individual Christians. Together they need to seek the anointing to break the yoke in their local areas. This is not simply a vision for church planting, Colin maintains.

'Harvest time isn't just spreading a few new churches but seeing a spiritual awakening in the land. We get the anointing, *God* breaks the yoke and the nation rejoices because it's harvest time. So we want people who are bold as lions, not mealy-mouthed mice!'

Revival will of course bring a hunger for lost souls, but in the meantime we can ask God for that hunger, the sense of their desolation.

'God's put you in the midst of a people hellbent, literally, on spiritual destruction. Your job, the most important you'll ever be given, is to pray for them,' believes Colin.

Once we grasp that, we begin to realise that every decision has eternal significance. This could be a decision not to talk to someone about Jesus; it does not affect our salvation, but it does affect the salvation of the person we have failed to help. Colin wants people to realise that every time they decide to sin, watch the wrong television programme or yield to judging and criticising, God will of course forgive them, but that sin, that failure to live according to His word, will have eternal significance.

In 1 John 2:18–28, John talks of it being the last hour. If two thousand years seems a long hour, all the more reason to believe that we really are in the end times now. As Colin told the Faith '92 audience, consisting of several thousand people from churches all over Britain, 'If we're alert to the things of the Spirit, we know God's building up to something so significant that we can't even imagine what it is.

'But the big question isn't *whether* it'll happen, but who will be involved in it. God waits till we get to the end of doing things our way and let Him do it His way.

'So what will happen? There'll be opposition, for a start. And the opposition which hurts most will be that within the Church. Opposition comes through comfortable Christianity – unbelief, fear and compromise. It'll come from people who seem the most well-meaning and sincere but who don't believe the truth. I was brought up in such a church where the people didn't know the truth and so couldn't believe it because they tried to use their reason and dilute the truth to match their so-called twentieth-century "rational" thinking. But if God is to have His way in the nation, it'll be done by the truth. In other words, Jesus is going to turn up. And we want such a move of God's Spirit that Jesus is being revealed all over the place.

'With the eyes of faith we must see the nation being restored to joy. This is a time when there will be a spiritual awakening in the nation.

'Count me in, Lord.'

> 'For we know, brothers loved by God, that he has chosen you, because our gospel came to you not simply with words, but also with power, with the Holy Spirit and with deep conviction. You know how we lived among you for your sake. You became imitators of us and of the Lord; in spite of severe suffering, you welcomed the message with the joy given by the Holy Spirit. And so you became a model to all the believers in Macedonia and Achaia. The Lord's message rang out from you not only in Macedonia and Achaia – your faith in God has become known everywhere.' (1 Thessalonians 1:4–8)

NOTES

Chapter One
1. Colin Whittaker, *Great Revivals*, London, Marshall Pickering, 1984.
2. R E Davies, *I Will Pour Out My Spirit*, Eastbourne, Monarch, 1992.
3. Colin Urquhart, *Faith for the Future*, London, Hodder & Stoughton, 1982.

Chapter Three
1. Colin Urquhart, *Listen and Live*, London, Hodder & Stoughton, 1987.
2. Colin Urquhart, *Holy Fire*, London, Hodder & Stoughton, 1984.

Chapter Four
1. Colin Urquhart, *When the Spirit Comes*, London, Hodder & Stoughton, 1974.
2. Caroline Urquhart, *His God, My God*, Guildford, Highland Books, 1983.

Chapter Five
1. Colin Urquhart, *My Dear Child*, London, Hodder & Stoughton, 1990, p 243.
2. Charles Sibthorpe, *A Man under Authority*, Eastbourne, Kingsway, 1984.
3. Colin Urquhart, *In Christ Jesus*, London, Hodder & Stoughton, 1981.
4. Colin Urquhart, *Holy Fire*, London, Hodder & Stoughton, 1984.

Chapter Six
1. This is also recorded by Bob Gordon, *Out of the Melting Pot*, London, Marshalls, 1984.

Chapter Seven
1. Colin Urquhart, *Listen and Live*, London, Hodder & Stoughton, 1987. There is a *Listen & Live* tape accompanying the book which is recommended because it leads one through this method of prayer and gives its scriptural basis.

Chapter Eight
1. *Jesus you are mighty*, copyright Colin Owen, 1991. Available on the *Proclaim Him* worship tape from Kingdom Faith Ministries. Sheet music also available.
2. English does not always convey the richness of Hebrew words. Certain words translated as 'dance' in most Bibles actually signify quite specific forms of dancing.
Old Testament Hebrew references:
Machol – dance, dancing, chorus:
Psalm 30:11, Psalm 149:3, Psalm 150:4, Jeremiah 31:4,13, Lamentations 5:15.
Mecholah – dance, dancing, chorus: Exodus 15:20, 32:19, Judges 11:34, Judges 21:21, 1 Samuel 18:6, 1 Samuel 21:11, 1 Samuel 29:5.
Chul (hull) – to dance by twisting and turning: Judges 21:23
New Testament Greek reference:
Choros – a chorus, company of dancers: Luke 15:25

Chapter Nine
1. Colin Urquhart, *Faith for the Future*, London, Hodder & Stoughton, 1982.
2. Colin Urquhart, *Receive your Healing*, London, Hodder & Stoughton, 1986.
3. This story is fully told in chapter 10 of Colin Urquhart's *Faith for the Future*, London, Hodder & Stoughton, 1982.
4. Colin Urquhart, *Anything You Ask*, London, Hodder & Stoughton, 1978.

If you would like to receive details of other Kingdom Faith books and teaching tapes by Colin Urquhart and Dan Chesney, or Kingdom Faith courses and conferences, including their annual Faith Camp, please write to:

Kingdom Faith Ministries
Roffey Place
Old Crawley Road
Faygate
HORSHAM
West Sussex
RH12 4SA

Tel: 0293 851543
Fax: 0293 851330